# CONFIDENTIALITY LIMITS IN PSYCHOTHERAPY

# Important Notice

The statements and opinions published in this book are the responsibility of the author. Such opinions and statements do not represent official policies, standards, guidelines, or ethical mandates of the American Psychological Association (APA), the APA Ethics Committee or Ethics Office, or any other APA governance group or staff. Statements made in this book neither add to nor reduce requirements of the APA "Ethical Principles of Psychologists and Code of Conduct" (2010), hereinafter referred to as the Ethics Code, nor can they be viewed as a definitive source of the meaning of the Ethics Code standards or their application to particular situations. Each ethics committee or other relevant body must interpret and apply the Ethics Code as it believes proper, given all the circumstances of each particular situation. Any information in this book involving legal and ethical issues should not be used as a substitute for obtaining personal legal and/or ethical advice and consultation prior to making decisions regarding individual circumstances.

# CONFIDENTIALITY LIMITS IN PSYCHOTHERAPY

## Ethics Checklists for Mental Health Professionals

Mary Alice Fisher

American Psychological Association • Washington, DC

Published by
American Psychological Association
750 First Street, NE
Washington, DC 20002
www.apa.org

To order
APA Order Department
P.O. Box 92984
Washington, DC 20090-2984
Tel: (800) 374-2721; Direct: (202) 336-5510
Fax: (202) 336-5502; TDD/TTY: (202) 336-6123
Online: www.apa.org/pubs/books
E-mail: order@apa.org

In the U.K., Europe, Africa, and the Middle East, copies may be ordered from
American Psychological Association
3 Henrietta Street
Covent Garden, London
WC2E 8LU England

Typeset in Minion by Circle Graphics, Inc., Columbia, MD

Printer: Sheridan Books, Chelsea, MI
Cover Designer: Mercury Publishing Services, Inc., Rockville, MD



**Library of Congress Cataloging-in-Publication Data**

Names: Fisher, Mary Alice, author.
Title: Confidentiality limits in psychotherapy : ethics checklists for mental health professionals / Mary Alice Fisher.
Description: Washington, DC : American Psychological Association, 2016. | Includes bibliographical references and index.
Identifiers: LCCN 2015036677 | ISBN 9781433821899 | ISBN 1433821893
Subjects: LCSH: Psychotherapist and patient—Moral and ethical aspects. | Confidential communications.
Classification: LCC RC480.8 .F56 2016 | DDC 616.89/14—dc23 LC record available at http://lccn.loc.gov/2015036677

**British Library Cataloguing-in-Publication Data**
A CIP record is available from the British Library.

*Printed in the United States of America*
*First Edition*

http://dx.doi.org/10.1037/14860-000

# Contents

# CONFIDENTIALITY LIMITS IN PSYCHOTHERAPY

# Introduction

John Goodman describes himself as a dedicated psychotherapist who considers his clients' interests to be paramount. He always begins his initial intake interviews by gently eliciting information from prospective clients, avoiding any "anxiety-provoking" discussion of the fact that the information they are about to share might not remain confidential. Yesterday, during an intake session, a prospective client asked him, "If I tell you what is really in my heart, do you promise to keep it a secret?" Reassured by Goodman's response about the importance of confidentiality in psychotherapy and taking this as a promise to protect her secrets, she talked at length about her fears and hopes, her past actions and future plans. By the end of the intake session, she had described two things Goodman later discovered he was legally required to report, and she had mentioned a pending court case in which he feared he might be ordered to testify. He knew this new client would feel betrayed if he disclosed the information she

http://dx.doi.org/10.1037/14860-001
*Confidentiality Limits in Psychotherapy: Ethics Checklists for Mental Health Professionals*, by M. A. Fisher

had shared with him, but he was also aware of the potential risks to her—and also to himself—if he did not.

Goodman slowly realized that by avoiding the initial discussion of "limits of confidentiality," he had not been protecting his clients; instead, he had been protecting himself from the discomfort of not knowing exactly what those limits might be. In the process, he had been depriving prospective clients of their right to be informed about the potential risks in advance—before they shared their secrets with him.[1]

This manual uses a checklist format and a step-by-step approach that is designed to help psychotherapists prepare to avoid the predictable pitfalls, handle practical challenges, and resolve ethical–legal dilemmas involving confidentiality. Most important, it is designed to ensure that the confidentiality rights of mental health clients will be respected, even when their confidences are not protectable.

We can be prepared to inform prospective clients accurately and honestly about how we intend to behave about confidentiality only if we have first carefully informed ourselves about our ethical and legal obligations and have decided what we really intend to do.

## DECIDING HOW TO PROTECT CLIENTS' CONFIDENTIALITY RIGHTS

Only two ethical options are available for protecting the confidentiality rights of therapy clients. Option 1 provides clients with absolute protection of their confidential information, but it is "illegal" in the sense that it would sometimes require civil disobedience. That is why almost all psychotherapists choose Option 2 instead. Option 2 protects psychotherapists from the risks involved in disobeying the law, but it leaves clients at risk of having their confidences disclosed. Option 2 therefore requires psychotherapists to take on the ethical responsibilities that are outlined in the following chapters of this manual.

[1] The vignettes in this manual are hypothetical. Although they contain some details that are drawn from actual cases, the specifics have been changed to disguise them.

## Option 1: Providing Absolute Confidentiality

This option exceeds the Ethical Standards[2] of every mental health profession (none of which ethically requires the unconditional protection of clients' confidences). This may make it an extremely "ethical" option, but it is definitely not a "legal" model of practice. Adopting Option 1 requires a willingness to break all laws that can require psychotherapists to disclose information and a willingness to accept the consequences of that action. The legal, financial, and personal consequences of promising absolute confidentiality can therefore be severe, which is why few psychotherapists choose Option 1 and why no mental health profession requires it. (For a detailed discussion of the potential risks, see Bollas & Sundelson, 1995.)

Those who advocate Option 1 nevertheless believe that its clinical advantages make it the only appropriate stance for those who take seriously the concept of the unconscious (see, e.g., Bollas & Langs, 1999; Bollas & Sundelson, 1995; Kipnis, 2003; Langs, 1998, 2008). In fact, some psychotherapists do promise their clients absolute confidentiality and actually keep that promise despite the risks to themselves. This includes "confidentiality heroes" such as Karen Beyer (2000), whose willingness to risk jail rather than breach client confidentiality led to a U.S. Supreme Court decision that expanded confidentiality protections in federal court cases (see *Jaffee v. Redmond*, 1996).

## Option 2: Providing Conditional Confidentiality and Protecting the Client's Right to Know the Conditions in Advance

This option meets the current Ethical Standards of every mental health profession, and most psychotherapists choose it to avoid the consequences of Option 1. However, this decision simply transfers the risks to their clients. Therefore, psychotherapists who choose Option 2 are ethically required to decide in advance when and in what respects they will limit their protection of clients' confidences. In other words, therapists

[2] In this manual, the term *Ethical Standards*, when capitalized, refers specifically to the enforceable standards contained in the ethics codes of mental health professionals. For a list of such ethics codes, see Appendix A. For definitions and clarifications of ethical and legal terms, see Appendix B.

must decide what limits of confidentiality will apply in their own practice and inform prospective clients about those limits in advance, before they share information that might later be disclosed without their consent. Otherwise, clients will enter the therapy relationship uninformed about those limits and will be unprotected.

Ethics codes give therapists the ethical freedom to disclose information without client consent when they are required by law to do so, as well as the ethical freedom to limit confidentiality by policy in certain other circumstances. But this ethical freedom to limit confidentiality is not "free." Therapists must "purchase" it by informing prospective clients about exactly when their confidences will not be protected and by obtaining their consent at intake to accept the risks (i.e., to accept the limits that will be imposed on confidentiality) as a condition of receiving services.

- *Psychotherapists who choose Option 1 will all behave the same way about confidentiality, whereas those who choose Option 2 may each have slightly different policies.* With Option 2, the list of limits of confidentiality—the circumstances in which the psychotherapist might later disclose information without obtaining the client's consent at the time—will vary across therapists and across settings. For clients, this means that the level of confidentiality offered by a previous therapist may be different from the next therapist. Therefore, therapists who choose Option 2 are responsible for devising a personalized description of how they will practice—a set of policies that can be described in terms simple enough for clients to understand, but presented in enough detail to allow them to predict foreseeable risks.
- *Psychotherapists who choose Option 1 must behave the same way in all circumstances, whereas therapists who choose Option 2 must make personal decisions about how they intend to behave in a wide range of "reasonably foreseeable" circumstances.* Option 2 involves making clear decisions and making them in advance, so the policies about confidentiality can be described to prospective clients at intake, before they give consent to receive services. Therapists are therefore not ethically free to "wing it" in the initial interview or to rely on ad hoc decision making about confidentiality because this would leave clients unwarned and unprotected. Unless

a specific limit of confidentiality has been explained to clients in advance, therapists are not ethically free to decide later to breach confidentiality simply because doing so would be personally or financially convenient at the time, or even because they deem it to be in the client's interest to do so.

- *Psychotherapists who choose Option 2 are not ethically free to use silence about confidentiality to imply a promise they do not intend to keep while eliciting information they might later decide they must disclose.* Clinicians who protect confidentiality unconditionally (Option 1) retain full clinical freedom to explore and interpret clients' concerns and fantasies about confidentiality while remaining silent indefinitely (if they so choose) about their real intentions, because the client's confidentiality is never actually at risk. However, clinicians who want to be free to make exceptions to confidentiality (Option 2) must provide prospective clients with an intelligible description of the exceptions "up front," and must provide accurate informational answers to clients' questions whenever they arise. That is because, for these clients, confidentiality is not "hypothetically" at risk but is actually at risk.
- *Psychotherapists who choose Option 2 must therefore be clear in advance, both with themselves and with their clients, about what their intentions really are.* This means they must not only decide what they should do in a variety of foreseeable situations—a difficult enough task—but they must also be prepared to give prospective clients an honest description of what they actually will do, which may be different.

In short, psychotherapists are ethically free to place conditions on confidentiality only if they protect the client's right to be informed in advance about what those conditions will be. This confidentiality right creates the ethical responsibilities described in this manual, especially the responsibilities about informed consent.

## WHY USE ETHICS-BASED CHECKLISTS?

First, the checklists in this book can serve as a reminder that there is no "Option 3." Psychotherapists are not ethically free to remain silent about the issue while postponing their policy decisions about confidentiality, nor are they ethically free to "ad lib" the discussion of limits of confidentiality because they have not decided what limits they might actually impose. Most psychotherapists do end up placing conditions on confidentiality, even if they wish they did not have to. Regrettably, many promise absolute confidentiality—or imply that promise by their silence—but then end up breaking their promise if they find themselves faced with legal consequences. However, it is unethical to promise more confidentiality than we would be willing to actually provide if it turned out that doing so placed us at risk. According to the ethics codes of our professions, it is also unethical to allow our silence on the matter to imply such a promise. We must therefore be prepared to inform prospective clients in advance about the conditions we actually intend to place on confidentiality, because failing to do so places them at risk.

Second, although the checklists in this manual can be helpful regardless of whether the psychotherapist chooses Option 1 or Option 2, they are especially important for those who choose Option 2, because of the many confidentiality decisions that must be made in advance. This includes most of today's mental health professionals. The decision to place limiting "conditions" on confidentiality brings some difficult and complicated ethical responsibilities. Those are noted in the first chapter and are outlined in detail in the checklists and discussions in the remaining six chapters of this manual. In the absence of a structure such as the checklists provide, it can be difficult for psychotherapists to be prepared to protect their clients' confidentiality rights.

Third, although this manual does not advocate civil disobedience, it does encourage psychotherapists to "reach for the ethical ceiling" by protecting confidentiality to the extent legally possible, even if their profession's ethics code would allow them to do less. "Ethics Codes create the 'ethical floor'—the minimum standards of behavior. But if we do no more than follow the minimum rules, we are missing the major point about confidentiality" (Fisher, 2013, p. 121). The ethical checklists require us to become clear about how much confidentiality protection we will actually be willing to provide. This involves clarity about the ethical and legal requirements, as well as personal soul-searching about how to translate those into clinical practice. The first checklist is the most difficult but also the most important because this preparation is essential to the protection of clients' rights.

Finally, and perhaps most important, this manual is written from an ethical perspective. At times, it necessarily refers to legal issues and sometimes it does reflect risk-management concerns, but the primary focus is on professional ethics—on protecting clients and their rights—not on legal obedience or therapist self-protection. Hopefully, this will help to reduce the unfortunate confusion between ethics and laws.

I believe that, regrettably, the ability of psychotherapists to protect the confidentiality rights of their clients has been progressively undermined by ethical–legal confusion. Ethical Standards about confidentiality and legal requirements about confidentiality are two different things, but mental health professionals easily confuse the two, and this places clients' rights at risk. Although some laws echo and support therapists' professional Ethical Standards, other laws can conflict with them, and this complicates matters. It further complicates ethical decision making if laws are taught in isolation in a manner that ignores their ethical implications.

In an attempt to cut through the resulting ethical–legal confusion, the six checklist chapters of this manual follow the six steps of an ethical practice model that takes an "ethics first" perspective. This model was constructed not from laws but from the confidentiality duties in psychotherapists' own ethics codes and professional guidelines. It therefore outlines ethical responsibilities about confidentiality in a manner that places laws into ethical perspective.

The complete ethical practice model is presented in the next chapter of this manual. The outline itself summarizes ethical obligations about confidentiality, as described in ethics codes for mental health professionals. To practice ethically about confidentiality, however, one must also consider how to respond to possible legal requirements—including state and federal laws that either protect confidentiality or require disclosure. The annotated version of the model in Appendix G (Center for Ethical Practice, 2010) integrates these ethical and legal obligations by beginning with an ethical context, then using italics to indicate how laws fit into this ethical picture.

In a 2008 article in *American Psychologist*, I advocated the use of such a model. I later elaborated on the model in an invited chapter entitled "Confidentiality and Record Keeping" in the *APA Handbook of Ethics in Psychology* (Fisher, 2012). Oxford University Press then published *The Ethics of Conditional Confidentiality*, a book based on that model (Fisher, 2013). This manual simplifies matters by using that six-step model to create six "checklists" that can be used first for advance planning, and then as a structure for following through with those plans and monitoring one's own practices. It is intended both as a handy desktop resource for practicing clinicians and as a teaching tool for professors, supervisors, and workshop leaders.

The model can be adapted for use in any setting and with any population (see examples of such adaptations at Center for Ethical Practice, 2014a). The following are the six steps listed in abbreviated form:

Step 1. Prepare to protect confidentiality rights.
Step 2. Tell clients the truth.
Step 3. Obtain consent before disclosing voluntarily.
Step 4. Respond ethically to legal demands.
Step 5. Avoid "avoidable" disclosures.
Step 6. Talk about confidentiality.

The first step is the only one not drawn directly from professional ethics codes, simply because this preparation is not emphasized there. Step 1 includes extensive preparation for the initial informed consent discussion with the client. It requires clarifying one's policies and preparing to inform prospective clients about the potential limits of confidentiality. It is therefore the most complex and time consuming of the six steps. It is nevertheless well worth the investment of time because of the ethically essential protection it provides to prospective therapy clients. Otherwise, we leave clients unable to protect themselves, unable to make an informed decision about whether to trust us with their secrets.

For each of the six steps in the model, this manual provides a separate chapter consisting of a checklist for you to work through and a discussion of the ethical issues involved at that step. Each chapter ends with a vignette that requires "Taking the Client's Perspective." This helps to maintain a focus on avoiding practices that place the client's confidences at risk, rather than focusing on our own convenience.

The ethical practice model on which this manual is based applies to all mental health professionals, regardless of their profession, practice setting, or theoretical orientation. It applies to all the therapeutic services provided by mental health professionals, regardless of whether they are described as counseling, therapy, psychotherapy, or psychoanalysis. At each step along the way, psychotherapists can encounter complications and dilemmas that require careful decision making. Formal decision-making models can provide a structure for the process of considering options and weighing potential consequences of possible actions. For using general ethical decision-making models at any step of the ethical practice model, readers can consult those provided elsewhere (see, e.g., Fisher, 2005; Forester-Miller & Davis, 1996; Haas & Malouf, 2005; Knapp & VandeCreek, 2012; Koocher & Keith-Spiegel, 2008; Mattison, 2000; Pope & Vasquez, 2011).

## SUGGESTIONS FOR USING THIS MANUAL

The first task, preparation, outlined in Step 1, involves some research about your profession's ethics code and your state's laws. For most states, the American Psychological Association has published reference books about relevant laws in its *Law & Mental Health Professionals Series* (e.g., *Law & Mental Health Professionals* for Virginia [Porfiri & Resnick, 2000] and Ohio [VandeCreek & Kapp, 2005]), but it is also important to obtain further legal information, as well as annual legal updates, from your state professional association.

The checklists make this appear to be a simple desk manual, but it contains much to consider, internalize, and implement. Although many busy therapists will use this manual independently, you are encouraged to consider working your way through it along with others, as a group, if you are able. If you do not already have a peer consultation group that could join you in implementing this project, this might be a good time to form a group of trusted colleagues for this purpose. Tackling the manual as a group project can also make it possible to review each other's personalized confidentiality forms, practice aloud what you want to say during the initial informed consent conversations about confidentiality, and provide ongoing consultation to each other when confidentiality dilemmas later arise.

Such a collaborative approach can also help mental health professionals avoid the hazards of becoming too isolated from colleagues and resources, which is an occupational hazard for psychotherapists. "Creating ways to stay in connection with others seems to be one of the most basic, important, and helpful self-care strategies" (Pope & Vasquez, 2005, p. 16). Creating such a group for ethical planning and support also brings other advantages, as discussed in the last chapter of this manual, "Step 6: Talk About Confidentiality."

This manual is appropriate for use in classrooms as a supplemental ethics text for clinical graduate students or as a desk manual in practicum and internship settings. It is equally useful as the basis for continuing education training in workshop or seminar settings for experienced psychotherapists.

As you proceed through these six checklists and review the materials in the appendices, you may discover that some of the ways you have practiced in the past have left the confidentiality rights of your psychotherapy clients unprotected. Perhaps your information sheets or informed consent forms created problems. Perhaps there are exceptions to confidentiality that are required in your setting but that you have failed to explain to clients in advance. Perhaps you will discover that the laws in your state have changed and that promises you previously made (or implied) can no longer be kept. As you consider making changes to your intake forms and client handouts, remember that informed consent is not a one-time event. It is never too late to reopen the conversation about confidentiality and its limits, to revise your intake forms to be sure they are consistent with your policies and with your state's laws, and to review your revised forms with current clients.

# The Ethical ABCs of Conditional Confidentiality

A. *Put the ethical rules first.*
B. *Learn the relevant laws.*
C. *Avoid ethical–legal confusion.*

These basic ethical rules look simple when you list them, but they can become complicated to put into practice.

## A. PUT THE ETHICAL RULES FIRST

Each mental health profession has an ethics code that contains Ethical Standards about confidentiality. In contrast to laws, these ethical obligations were devised by your own profession and are enforceable for members of national professional associations. Even if you are not a member,

http://dx.doi.org/10.1037/14860-002
*Confidentiality Limits in Psychotherapy: Ethics Checklists for Mental Health Professionals*, by M. A. Fisher

these standards reflect the ethical behavior expected for practitioners of your profession, so we suggest that you keep a copy of your profession's ethics code in the back of this manual (if you do not have one, see Appendix A, download a copy, and consider obtaining a recent ethics text).

Ethics codes define the minimum standards—the "ethical floor" of your behavior about confidentiality—but you are free to "reach for the ethical ceiling" by adopting personal standards that are even more client protective than your profession's ethics code (see Appendix B for definitions and clarifications of these and other terms).

- *Know the ethical rules of your own profession.* These include not only ethical standards about maintaining confidences but also the related ethical obligations about informed consent. As you read your ethics code, keep your eye out for the Ethical Standards that can affect clients' confidentiality rights without even containing the word *confidentiality.*
- *Make promises carefully.* A promise of "absolute" or "unconditional" confidentiality may reassure prospective clients, but it creates both ethical and legal complications. It would be unethical to make that promise and then fail to keep it, but keeping that promise can be illegal if it leads you to disobey laws that require you to disclose information without the client's consent. Almost all psychotherapists avoid this civil disobedience by promising only "conditional" confidentiality instead. That promise is easier to keep because it allows psychotherapists to obey the law, but it does bring its own complications. You can live up to your ethical obligations about conditional confidentiality only if you first take the time to prepare carefully, as described in Step 1 of the confidentiality practice model.
- *Remember that placing limits on confidentiality creates informed consent obligations.* Placing "limiting conditions" on your confidentiality promise creates an ethical obligation to inform prospective clients about what those conditions will be. This informed consent conversation about the limits of confidentiality should take place before clients confide things you might later disclose to others without their consent.

To enter this initial informed consent conversation adequately prepared, you must decide in advance exactly which conditions you intend to impose on confidentiality. That preparation includes informing yourself about your ethical and legal obligations, deciding in advance what limits you will impose on confidentiality, and preparing to explain when you might actually breach confidentiality in the future. Only then will you be ready to inform prospective clients accurately and honestly and to avoid promising (or by silence, implying) more confidentiality protections than you will actually be willing or able to provide.

You are then free to obtain clients' consent to receive your services on that basis. Within the ethical practice model, the checklists in Step 1 can guide you through the necessary preparation; then the checklists in Step 2 can guide you through the ethically required informed consent discussion with prospective clients about confidentiality and its limits.

Note that obtaining a prospective client's informed consent to enter a psychotherapy relationship requires more than obtaining a signature on a consent form. Before giving consent to receive services, clients must be informed about the risks, including the possibility that the information they share during psychotherapy might later be disclosed without their consent. Ethically, that conversation is important because it gives clients their first (and sometimes their only) opportunity to protect themselves from unexpected breaches of confidentiality by knowing in advance when you will breach confidentiality and when you will not.

*Thereafter, obtain the client's explicit consent before disclosing anything voluntarily.* Any time you disclose client information when you are not legally compelled to do so, you are disclosing "voluntarily." At Step 2, you obtain the client's informed consent for potential voluntary disclosures that would apply to all clients; then at Step 3 you must obtain the informed client's consent for client-specific disclosures. In both situations, it is important to remember that obtaining "truly informed" consent means obtaining "consent from an informed person," not just obtaining a signature on a form. For example, this involves informing the client about what information you will be disclosing and to whom, as well as the potential implications of disclosing or not disclosing it, before obtaining the client's written consent to share information with others.

*Be prepared to protect confidentiality to the extent legally possible.* This involves learning to respond ethically when you are confronted with laws that legally require you to disclose client information "involuntarily" (i.e., whether or not you wish to, and whether or not the client gives consent). Such laws can create specific ethical responsibilities, and Step 4 contains checklists for responding ethically to these legal demands. You must also distinguish between actions that are legally required and those that are merely legally allowed (see the definitions in Appendix B). Ethically speaking, laws that merely allow disclosures are different from laws that require you to disclose information. The fact that you are sometimes legally allowed to disclose something without the client's consent does not necessarily make it ethical to make that disclosure without consent. Disclosures that are merely legally allowed are *voluntary* disclosures—meaning the client is free *not* to give consent, and you are legally free *not* to disclose—so if you intend to disclose in certain circumstances, the best protection for clients involves obtaining their consent first, either in the initial informed consent conversation (Step 2) or later (Step 3).

Step 5 contains checklists that deal with "avoidable" voluntary disclosures; it involves an understanding of which disclosures are sometimes preventable even in legal contexts. Finally, the Step 6 checklists help you create relationships in which the topic of confidentiality can be safely discussed with others for their education, for mutual support in the midst of confidentiality dilemmas, and for lobbying for better legal protection of confidentiality where that is needed.

## B. LEARN THE RELEVANT LAWS

Taking an ethics-first perspective does not mean you can ignore the laws that affect your ability to protect confidences. Unlike Ethical Standards that arise within your own profession, the laws that affect confidentiality were enacted by legislators or regulators or were created by court decisions. These laws, which can originate at either the state or federal level, are of two major types: Laws that help you protect confidentiality and laws that limit confidentiality. It further confuses matters that some laws actually do both. (Appendix C describes types of laws that can affect your ability to protect confidentiality. For examples of each type of law and links to their texts, see http://www.centerforethicalpractice.org/lawsaffectingconfidentiality.)

- *Learn your state laws.* Laws that require you to disclose client information usually arise at the state level. These laws have the most direct impact on your ability to protect client confidences. The relevant laws vary greatly from state to state, and you are responsible for learning the laws of your own state. Therapists who have trained or practiced in one state must take the time to learn a new set of laws if they move to another state.

  In organizing your state's laws, you might consider using categories such as those in Appendix C. It can be helpful to create a chart of such laws for your own state (see, e.g., a chart of Virginia laws affecting confidentiality, with links to the text of each law, at http://www.centerforethicalpractice.org/lawsaffectingconfidentiality). The ethical practice model used in this manual can be helpful when creating such a chart for your own state and can be useful when planning how to respond ethically to each of these types of laws.
- *Know which federal laws apply to you.* Federal laws apply nationwide, but some apply only in certain settings. The most prominent federal laws affecting confidentiality arise from the Health Insurance Portability and Accountability Act of 1996 (HIPAA) regulations, which apply in any setting that transmits client information electronically. Most other federal laws apply only in certain settings (e.g., in schools or in federally funded substance abuse treatment facilities). In federal court cases, the Federal Rules of Evidence (Federal Evidence Review, 2015) will apply, in contrast to the state privilege laws that apply in state court cases.
- *Distinguish between* voluntary *disclosures and* legally required *disclosures.* Ethically speaking, this is an important distinction. According to your ethics code, you are ethically responsible for informing prospective clients about any foreseeable limits of confidentiality, which would include both voluntary and involuntary disclosures (Step 2), for obtaining the client's informed consent before you make any subsequent voluntary disclosure (Step 3), and for responding ethically when faced with a legal demand for involuntary disclosure of information

(Step 4). Legally speaking, this is also an important distinction. You are legally responsible for knowing when your laws require you to disclose something (e.g., report child abuse), and sometimes there are legal penalties for failing to do so. But if you disclose without the client's consent when you are *not* legally required to, there can also sometimes be penalties—both ethical penalties and legal penalties.

- *Distinguish between* legally required *disclosures and* legally allowed *disclosures.* Legally speaking, laws that require you to disclose client information are different from laws that merely "allow" you to disclose. Ethically speaking, a legally allowed disclosure is a voluntary disclosure (meaning that the client remains free not to give consent and the therapist remains free not to disclose), and before you are ethically free to disclose voluntarily, you must obtain consent (Fisher, 2013). (This ethically important distinction was discussed earlier.)

## C. AVOID ETHICAL–LEGAL CONFUSION

When psychotherapists confuse legal requirements with ethical obligations, they are more likely to place clients' confidentiality rights at risk. It is important to know the difference between the two—and to notice when they come into conflict—because therapists have certain ethical responsibilities when their laws conflict with their profession's Ethical Standards.

- *Remember to take an "ethics first" approach about confidentiality.* Your ethics code describes your responsibilities as defined by your profession, which is why they were placed first in the ABC summary at the beginning of this chapter. This is where you should begin when making decisions about confidentiality because these standards represent the ethical floor of your profession—the minimum standards below which you may not fall. But you need not settle for that "floor." The checklists in the following six chapters are designed to help you reach for the ethical ceiling about confidentiality to protect clients' confidentiality rights to the extent legally possible in your state.
- *Remember that laws sometimes support your Ethical Standards, but sometimes conflict with them.* When the two overlap, you can use those

protective laws on the behalf of clients whenever you are arguing for protection of their confidences. When they conflict, you must notice that you are facing an ethical–legal conflict because in that circumstance you have certain ethical obligations about what to do. These are summarized in Step 4 (Appendix C describes types of laws protective and unprotective of confidentiality).

- *Place laws into ethical perspective and keep them there.* The six-step ethical practice model on which this manual is based is an outline of our ethical responsibilities about confidentiality. As noted in the Introduction, the version of the model in Appendix G uses italics to indicate how laws fit into this ethical structure. This can serve as a reminder that laws have ethical implications. By showing how laws can fit into each ethical step, the model both helps you place your own state's laws into ethical context and helps you remember to keep them there. It leads you through the steps for preparing to recognize your state laws that can affect client confidentiality, learning how to use the laws that are protective of confidentiality, and establishing clear policies for responding to the laws that are unprotective of confidentiality or require you to limit it.
- *Plan how you will use each of the protective laws for better protection of the confidentiality of your clients.* For example, if you receive a legal demand to disclose confidential client information, you can cite both your profession's Ethical Standards and your state's nondisclosure laws as a basis for protecting the information from disclosure.
- *Plan how you will respond* ethically *to each of the laws that conflict with your ethics code or conflict with your own personal values about protecting clients' confidences.* When faced with laws that command you to breach confidentiality, you have certain ethical obligations about protecting a client's rights, and these are reflected in the ethical practice model. In Step 1, you must learn such laws in advance and decide how you will respond to them, so you will be prepared to describe your intentions accurately to prospective clients at intake at Step 2. Then at Step 4, you must respond ethically to legal demands when they arise. Step 5 is a reminder that failure to respond ethically to legal demands can result in disclosures that could have been prevented.

Finally, Step 6 offers ideas for pooling resources with other professionals for learning laws, planning how to respond to them, and lobbying for legislative reform when that is needed. It is impossible for us to have effective communication about confidentiality with each other or with others unless we all speak in the same language about it. Appendix B contains definitions of some words and phrases that will be used in this manual. These concepts are important for understanding confidentiality ethics and for discussing the issues clearly with each other and with others.

## ETHICALLY PERMITTED "DOORS" TO DISCLOSURE OF CONFIDENTIAL INFORMATION

Figure 1 uses the metaphor of "ethical doors" to illustrate when mental health professionals are ethically free to disclose client information and when they are not. This graphic reflects our client-protective recommendation that psychotherapists disclose information without consent only if legally compelled. The client's consent can be obtained at intake during the initial informed consent conversation or at any time thereafter (Step 2).

Door 1 is opened at intake through the initial informed consent conversation, and that door remains open throughout the relationship. A therapist who intends to place any limits on confidentiality is ethically required to inform prospective clients at intake and obtain their consent to accept those "limits of confidentiality" as a condition of receiving services. In other words, Door 1 is open only if the therapist explained during the initial interview that this particular disclosure might be made without the client's further consent. This conversation about foreseeable limits of confidentiality should include both (a) disclosures the therapist can be legally required to make, as well as (b) disclosures the therapist might voluntarily make without obtaining further client consent (see Appendix D for an outline of a sample client handout for this conversation). In this way, when giving consent to receive services, the informed client is giving consent to accept the described limits of confidentiality as a condition of receiving those services. This informed consent process allows clients to exercise their right to give "informed refusal" of services instead or to

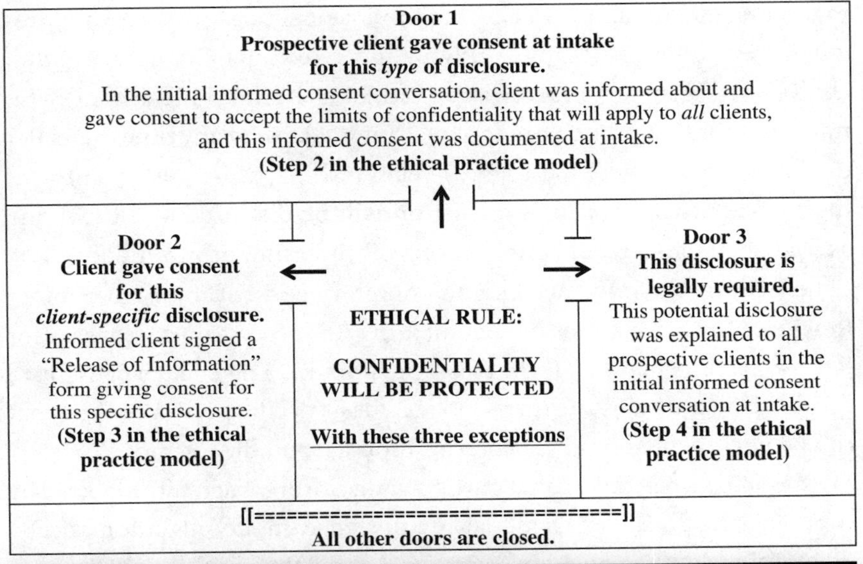


**Figure 1**

Ethically permitted "doors" to disclosure of confidential information. Based on the disclosure metaphor in Behnke (2004). From *The Ethics of Conditional Confidentiality: A Practice Model for Mental Health Professionals* (p. 12), by M. A. Fisher, 2013, New York, NY: Oxford University Press. Copyright 2013 by Oxford University Press. Adapted with permission.

limit what they reveal. Clients are best protected if this conversation happens before they begin to share information that might later be disclosed. This conversation should then be repeated later as appropriate (e.g., if the client seems to have forgotten what the rules are or if changes in laws or policies could affect confidentiality). (Note that the HIPAA "Final Rule" [2013] requires that the "Notice of Privacy Practices" contain a statement informing prospective clients that any disclosures not discussed there in advance will be made only with the client's consent.)

Door 2 is opened when the therapist obtains consent for disclosures that are specific to the particular client. Whereas the initial informed consent conversation describes the limits of confidentiality that will apply to all clients, this conversation obtains consent for a voluntary disclosure specific to this client. For example, this can include obtaining consent to discuss information with another professional (e.g., primary care provider, medical specialist), a family member (e.g., parent, spouse, adult child), or an agency (e.g., social services, mental health clinic, school). This informed consent process can take place at intake or at any time thereafter during (or even after) the therapy relationship. It involves (a) informing the client about what information will be disclosed and to whom, as well as the foreseeable implications of disclosing or not disclosing it; (b) obtaining the informed client's voluntary consent to disclose under those circumstances; and (c) documenting this process on a "Consent for Release of Information" form (see Appendix E). The client's consent to this particular disclosure opens Door 2 for a specific period of time that can be documented by using an expiration date on the form.

Door 3 is open only if that particular disclosure is actually required by some law. Legally speaking, in that circumstance this door is automatically open. Ethically speaking, however, consent for these disclosures is actually obtained in advance through Door 1 by informing prospective clients about the possibility of these potential legally imposed breaches of confidentiality. The therapist will then be ethically free to walk through Door 3 if there is no legal alternative. This ethical freedom arises not because the disclosure is legally required, but because the client was informed about and gave consent in advance to accept such a disclosure as a condition of receiving services.

Note that Door 3 is not open for making disclosures that are merely "legally allowed" but not legally required. The terms may sound similar, but ethically speaking they are very different, as reflected in the definitions in Appendix B and as demonstrated by the fact that they are discussed in this manual in two different chapters. Legally allowed disclosures are voluntary disclosures, so the most ethically appropriate path for such disclosures is through Door 1—obtaining the client's informed consent in advance for any legally allowed disclosures the therapist intends to make. Otherwise, therapists should obtain the client's explicit consent for such disclosures at the time they are made, thereby opening Door 2. This client-protective recommendation goes beyond the requirements in some ethics codes, and it definitely exceeds the legal standards in the federal HIPAA regulations, which allow many disclosures without client authorization.

Finally, the ethical practice model that I introduced in 2008 forms the outline for the six chapters of this manual. It is an ethics-based model because it was developed using the requirements in the ethics codes and guidelines of the mental health professions themselves. This model outlines the ethical behaviors required for protecting the confidentiality rights of those who receive mental health services in any setting.

Because it can be easy to confuse ethical requirements with legal requirements, an annotated version of the ethical practice model is provided in Appendix G, using italics to illustrate how *laws affecting confidentiality* fit into this ethics-based framework. Each step of the model contains guidelines for keeping laws in ethical perspective, so the ethical structure of the ethical practice model can be useful in planning how to respond ethically to each type of law that is unprotective of confidentiality. Exhibit 1 summarizes the ethical practice model.

**Exhibit 1**

**Protecting Clients' Confidentiality Rights: An Ethical Practice Model**

**Step 1: Prepare**

1. Understand clients' rights and your ethical responsibilities on behalf of those rights.
2. Learn laws affecting confidentiality (refer to Step 4).
3. Clarify your own personal ethical position about confidentiality and its limits. Decide when you will disclose client information "voluntarily." Plan your response to each law that can require you to disclose "involuntarily."
4. Find reliable ethics consultants and legal consultants and use them as needed.
5. Devise informed consent forms that reflect your actual policies and intentions.
6. Prepare to discuss confidentiality and its limits with patients in understandable language.

(*continues*)

## Exhibit 1

**Protecting Clients' Confidentiality Rights: An Ethical Practice Mode (*Continued*)**

### Step 2: Tell Prospective Clients the Truth (Inform Their Consent)

1. Inform prospective clients about limits of confidentiality that apply to all clients.
2. Explain any roles or potential conflicts of interest that might affect confidentiality.
3. Obtain the informed client's consent to accept these potential limits of confidentiality.
   - Inform prospective clients of potential "conditions" on confidentiality.
   - Obtain client consent to accept these as condition of receiving services.
   - Document this informed consent process.
4. Reopen the conversation if the client's circumstances, laws, or your intentions change.

### Step 3: Obtain "Truly Informed Consent" Before Disclosing Voluntarily

1. Disclose information without client consent only if legally unavoidable.
2. Inform clients adequately about the nature and implications of the proposed disclosure.
3. Obtain and document the client's signed consent before disclosing the information.

### Step 4: Respond Ethically to Legal Demands for Information

1. Notify clients of a pending legal requirement to disclose information without client consent.
2. Respond ethically to legal obligations (according to plan devised in Step 1).
3. Limit disclosure to the extent legally possible.

## Exhibit 1

**Protecting Clients' Confidentiality Rights: An Ethical Practice Mode (*Continued*)**

### Step 5: Avoid Preventable Breaches of Confidentiality

1. Establish and maintain protective policies and procedures in the office, institution, or agency.
2. Avoid "informal" discussions, "unofficial" disclosures, and casual conversations about clients.
3. Monitor record-keeping practices.
4. Avoid dual roles that create conflicts of interest in the courtroom and elsewhere.
5. Anticipate legal demands and empower clients to act protectively on their own behalf.
6. Do not confuse laws that *permit* disclosure with laws that legally *require* disclosure.

### Step 6: Talk About Confidentiality: Educate Each Other and Others

1. Go public: Refuse to keep confidentiality problems a secret.
2. Model ethical practices: Confront others' unethical practices.
3. Teach ethical practices to employees, students, supervisees, and agency administrators.
4. Educate attorneys, judges, and the public about the importance of confidentiality in therapy.
5. Explore possibilities for legislative change toward more protective confidentiality laws.
6. Develop multidisciplinary training, continuing education, and consultation.

*Note.* Adapted from "Protecting Confidentiality Rights: The Need for an Ethical Practice Model," by M. A. Fisher, 2008, *American Psychologist*, *63*, p. 7. Copyright 2008 by the American Psychological Association.

# Step 1. Prepare to Protect Confidentiality Rights

Understand Clients' Rights and My Ethical Responsibilities on Behalf of Those Rights.

- ☐ Learn my profession's ethical rules about confidentiality (use ethics code).
- ☐ Learn my profession's ethical rules about informed consent (use ethics code).
- ☐ Learn other professional guidelines about confidentiality and informed consent.
- ☐ Learn professional guidelines about responding to ethical–legal conflicts.

http://dx.doi.org/10.1037/14860-003
*Confidentiality Limits in Psychotherapy: Ethics Checklists for Mental Health Professionals*, by M. A. Fisher

## RESOURCES

Obtain a copy of the ethics code of my profession (see Appendix A).
Learn Ethical Standards about confidentiality and informed consent.
Choose a good ethics text; keep it on my desk (see Appendix A for a list).
Review the ethical practice model (in Exhibit 1 and in Appendix G).
Preview Step 4 for resources and references about ethical and legal conflicts.

Learn the Laws Affecting Confidentiality.

- ☐ Learn which state laws can help me protect client confidentiality.
  - ☐ Prepare to use them to advocate for the protection of clients' confidences.
- ☐ Learn which state laws can limit my ability to protect confidences.
  - ☐ If I plan to obey them, prepare to inform clients about this in advance.
  - ☐ If I plan to disobey them, prepare to accept penalties for civil disobedience.
- ☐ Learn federal laws that affect confidentiality (e.g., HIPAA Regulations).
- ☐ Make and regularly update a list of laws that affect confidentiality in my practice.

## RESOURCES

See Appendix C for laws that can protect or limit confidentiality, including HIPAA.
See "Examples of Federal and State Laws Affecting Confidentiality" (Center for Ethical Practice, 2013).
For state laws, contact my state professional association for a list of relevant laws.
See HIPAA links at http://www.centerforethicalpractice.org/links-to-HIPAA-resources

Clarify My Own Personal Ethical Position About Confidentiality and Its Limits.

- ☐ Using Appendix D, make a list of when (and to whom) I might disclose client information, whether "voluntarily" or "involuntarily."
- ☐ Using Appendix C and later chapters of this manual (especially Step 4), plan my response to each law that can limit confidentiality.
  - ☐ Laws requiring therapists to initiate disclosures (e.g., reporting laws)
  - ☐ Laws granting others access to client information without consent
  - ☐ Laws allowing recipients of information to redisclose without consent
  - ☐ Exceptions to therapist–client privilege in court cases

Note that for many mental health professionals, Step 1 is the most difficult step, because it requires both personal soul-searching and ethical decision making. It can be helpful to join with others who are undertaking this process, even though the end result may be slightly different for each person.

## RESOURCES

Consult the list of my own state laws from the previous checklist.

Decide how I intend to respond ethically to each state law that can require me to disclose information without a client's consent.

Read relevant articles and/or textbook chapters from reference list.

Discuss my position about each law with ethical/legal consultants.

Find Reliable Ethics Consultants and Legal Consultants and Use Them as Needed.

- ☐ Ethics consultants
- ☐ Legal consultants

## RESOURCES

Ask colleagues or professional associations to recommend ethics consultants.

Seek referrals for attorneys familiar with mental health law.

Contact potential consultants now; do not wait for a crisis.

Devise Clear Written Policies About Confidentiality and Enforce Those in My Setting.

- ☐ Devise intake forms that reflect my actual policies and intentions about confidentiality (e.g., informed consent forms; personalized HIPAA-compliant "Notice of Privacy Practices").
- ☐ Create a simple list of "Limits of Confidentiality" for prospective clients (see Appendix D).
- ☐ Create one-way and two-way "Consent for Release of Information" forms for voluntary client-specific disclosures (see Appendix E).
- ☐ Provide ethics-based training about confidentiality for both clinical and nonclinical staff.

## RESOURCES

Use Appendices D and F to review my handouts for informing prospective clients. If using forms devised by others, adapt them to reflect my own intentions in my setting.

Obtain advice and support from colleagues when creating forms.

Seek colleagues' reactions to the "readability" of my forms. Have consultants review my forms for ethical and legal compliance.

See Appendix E for elements in a "Release of Information" form.

For planning ethics-based training, see Step 5, "Avoiding Preventable Disclosures."

Prepare to Discuss Confidentiality and Its Limits With Clients in Understandable Language.

- ☐ Prepare a written one-sheet bulleted summary of confidentiality's limits.
- ☐ Practice how I will review the written list with clients to test their understanding.
- ☐ Practice and learn to discuss limits of confidentiality without sounding uncertain, defensive or apologetic.

## RESOURCES

Using Appendix D, devise a bulleted summary of potential limits of confidentiality. Seek others' reactions to the "readability" of my initial informed consent handout.

Practice aloud—it helps to hear myself describe my own policies about confidentiality.

Have trusted peers critique my "nondefensive" posture in presenting the information.

## DISCUSSION

Ordinarily, ethical obligations toward a client will begin when the relationship begins. This is not the case with confidentiality. In today's legal climate, protection of confidentiality rights must begin before the prospective client ever enters the room because informed consent rights about confidentiality can be protected only if some difficult decisions have been made in advance. This was not always necessary. When psychotherapists and counselors faced no external impediments to protecting clients' secrets, they needed no special preparation for protecting clients' rights about confidentiality (Fisher, 2006). But once it became legally impossible for mental health professionals to protect clients' confidences without exception, protecting their confidentiality rights became exceedingly more complicated (Donner, VandeCreek, Gonsiorek, & Fisher, 2008; Fisher, 2012; Knapp, Gottlieb, Berman, & Handelsman, 2007; Pope & Bajt, 1988). Faced with legal demands for client information (and often committed to managed care contracts that allow others to obtain access to client records), therapists can no longer conduct clinical intakes ethically without first preparing to conduct them ethically.

It is hard to overestimate the importance of this forethought and planning. "Anticipation of ethical pitfalls and consultation with colleagues are key to preventing practitioners' most common ethical dilemmas" (Bailey, 2003, p. 68). Choose a good ethics text (see Appendix A) and find good ethics consultants. It can be ethically important to choose one's consultants carefully (Harris & Younggren, 2011) and to obtain the client's consent if any identifiable information will be shared during the consultation.

As reflected in the checklists presented earlier, the necessary preparation about confidentiality can be extensive. But we can be honest with a prospective client about our intentions only after we have decided what our intentions really are, and we cannot possibly know our intentions until we decide what limits might be imposed on confidentiality, whether imposed by our own policies in our private practice, by the requirements of our agency or group practice setting, or by the laws of our state.

Regrettably, this necessity for preparation is not usually emphasized during clinical training, so some therapists and counselors engage in clinical practice for years without ever developing clear policies about confidentiality or without learning to describe the potential limits of confidentiality clearly enough to be understood by prospective clients. Too often, unprepared psychotherapists will disclose client information unexpectedly if they face a situation in which withholding it would place them at risk. But this leaves their clients at risk. When clients believe that their confidences are more protected than they actually are, they may confide information that may later be disclosed unexpectedly if protecting it places the therapist at risk.

If you provide services in multi-client cases (e.g., couple, family, or group therapy), give careful consideration to exactly what the confidentiality policies will be for each involved party. For example, in family therapy, not everyone will be receiving the same promises about confidentiality, because the rules that apply to minors will be different from those for their parents. In couple therapy, both individuals have the same confidentiality rights, and you must be prepared to explain in advance how you will handle information you receive from one when the other is not present.

Therapists sometimes involve nonclient individuals who serve as "collateral" participants in someone else's therapy. This can include parents who receive consultations about a child therapy client, or can include a spouse or adult child who participates in therapy sessions with the consent of the client. The Trust (formerly the American Psychological Association [APA] Insurance Trust) provides a helpful form, "Sample Outpatient Services Agreement for Collaterals" (The Trust, 2006), which explains the rights of collateral participants and informs them that they do not have the same confidentiality rights as the client.

Helpful recommendations are available in recent ethics texts (see Appendix A). For detailed consideration of ethical and clinical issues in couple cases, also see sample policies by Kuo (2009) and Weeks, Odell, and Methven (2005). For multiple-party cases, see Fisher (2013, pp. 151–162). For risk-management considerations, see Bennett et al. (2006).

Ethics codes require that your description of "limits of confidentiality" be intelligible to the client. Psychologists must present the information in "language that is reasonably understandable" to the client (APA Ethical Standard 3.10a, "Informed Consent"). Marriage and family therapists have the same requirement (American Association for Marriage and Family Therapy Ethical Standard 1.2, "Informed Consent"). Social workers "should use clear and understandable language to inform clients" (National Association of Social Workers Ethical Standard 1.03). Counselors are expected to "communicate information in ways that are both developmentally and culturally appropriate" and to "use clear and understandable language when discussing issues related to informed consent" (American Counseling Association Ethical Standard 4.2.3, "Developmental and Cultural Sensitivity"). Research has indicated that many informed consent forms do not meet this ethical requirement (Handelsman, Kemper, Kesson-Craig, McLain, & Johnsrud, 1986; Handelsman & Martin, 1992; Wagner, Davis, & Handelsman, 1998) and that Health Insurance Portability and Accountability Act of 1996 (HIPAA) type forms are often not easily intelligible to the average therapy client, with most falling within the "difficult range of readability" (Walfish & Ducey, 2007, p. 204).

Most ethics codes do not require therapists to present the limits of confidentiality in writing, but the federal HIPAA regulations do legally require that prospective clients receive a written "Notice of Privacy Practices." As suggested in the risk-management literature, a written document not only protects clients but also protects the therapist (Bennett et al., 2006) by providing evidence of what promises were actually made.

Confidentiality is not the only topic that psychotherapists must cover in their initial informed consent discussion,[1] and information about the topic of confidentiality can easily be lost in a long document. Appendix D contains a sample document that can be used for listing the potential limits of confidentiality in a simple format that is much more client friendly than the legally required HIPAA "Notice of Privacy Practices." The Trust provides an additional informed consent document (Harris & Bennett, 1999)—a psychotherapist–client agreement that is "more user-friendly and much more relevant to psychotherapy" than the HIPAA document (Bennett et al., 2006, p. 114). Other sample informed consent forms are available online (see Center for Ethical Practice: http://www.centerforethicalpractice.org/ethical-legal-resources/links; Ken Pope: http://kspope.com/consent/index.php; and the Zur Institute: http://www.zurinstitute.com/forms.html). However,

[1] The Center for Ethical Practice provides a chart listing the informed consent topics ethically required for each mental health profession at http://www.centerforethicalpractice.org/ethical-legal-resources/ethical-information/

it is important to remember that no "canned" forms will suffice; you must edit them to ensure that the description of limits of confidentiality accurately reflects how you actually intend to behave in your own setting.

A written document that describes confidentiality policies can serve several purposes. First, the process of writing it serves as a self-test. Therapists who are unable to write their policies clearly probably are also unlikely to be able to say them clearly either, whether when explaining the confidentiality limits to prospective clients at intake or when answering questions later. Furthermore, therapists who are unclear about their own policies are unlikely to have consistent practices regarding confidentiality or enforce compliance with them by staff and others in the setting. Second, a written policy statement serves as both a reminder and documentation: This permanent evidence of what the therapist said about confidentiality can forestall later disputes about what was promised (Fisher, 2013). Appendix D can be used for creating such a written document.

Important decisions are made during this preparation process, and your written statement should accurately reflect those decisions. It is not only ethically important that the written policy statement be tailored to reflect the therapist's actual intentions but it is also legally important. The HIPAA "Final Rule" (2013) now requires that the "Notice of Privacy Practices" contain the following promise: "*Other uses and disclosures not described in the Notice of Privacy Practices will be made only with authorization from the individual* [emphasis added]" (p. 5623). In other words, before psychotherapists may make any disclosure about which clients were not forewarned, they must obtain the client's explicit consent to release the information. This new legal requirement is consistent with professional ethical standards and with recommendations in this manual as reflected in the Introduction.

This step has explored some of the preparation required for protecting the confidentiality rights of psychotherapy clients. The following vignette illustrates the importance of keeping the client's perspective in mind throughout this preparation.

## TAKING THE CLIENT'S PERSPECTIVE AT STEP 1: THE CASE OF THE UNPREPARED THERAPIST

At intake, your therapist did not mention confidentiality. At the next session, you decided to ask about it. The therapist explored your concerns and helped you talk about early childhood invasions of your privacy. He then asserted his personal belief in the importance of confidentiality to the therapy process. Reassured by this discussion, you disclosed a great deal of personal information that could be damaging to you if ever disclosed.

Six months into treatment, your therapist told you he had just reported something you told him. His explanation was that he only recently learned that he might incur a legal penalty for failure to report such information, and he feared that not reporting it would come to light. When asked why he did not discuss this with you before reporting, he replied, "This report was not optional, it was legally required, so it was not something we could decide together. There was no way to avoid it." You later discovered that, in fact, providers of his profession are not legally required to make this particular report.

In such circumstances, would you consider your rights protected by this unprepared and uninformed therapist?

# Step 2. Tell Prospective Clients the Truth About Foreseeable Limits of Confidentiality

Inform Prospective Clients About Limits of Confidentiality That Apply to All Clients.

- ☐ Begin the conversation before the client shares information I might have to disclose.
- ☐ Include disclosures I may make voluntarily.
- ☐ Include disclosures I may be legally required to initiate (e.g., abuse reports).
- ☐ Include other potential legally imposed limits of confidentiality.
- ☐ Include potential limits of confidentiality created by the use of technology.
- ☐ For couple, family, or group therapy, discuss rules about shared information.

http://dx.doi.org/10.1037/14860-004
*Confidentiality Limits in Psychotherapy: Ethics Checklists for Mental Health Professionals*, by M. A. Fisher

## RESOURCES

Review and use my checklists, forms, and resources from Step 1.
Review my client handout (see Appendix D).
If I am reluctant to "tell it all," practice some more!

Explain Any Roles or Potential Conflicts of Interest That Might Affect Confidentiality.

- ☐ Describe existing roles that may affect my ability to maintain confidentiality.
- ☐ Describe existing relationships or affiliations that may limit confidentiality.

## RESOURCES

Conversations such as those described in the previous chapter can help me prepare here.

Obtain Each Informed Client's Consent to Accept the Potential Limits of Confidentiality.

- ☐ Inform prospective clients of potential "conditions" on confidentiality.
- ☐ Obtain informed clients' consent to accept these limits of confidentiality as a condition of receiving services.
- ☐ Document this informed consent process.

## RESOURCES

See the following discussion and the reference list. Allow ample time for discussion; do not shortcut the informed consent process.

Reopen the Conversation If Clients' Circumstances, Laws, or My Intentions Change.

- ☐ Reopen as necessary to remind clients of these "conditions."
- ☐ Inform clients if changes in laws have changed my disclosure policies.
- ☐ Inform clients if my "voluntary disclosure" policies change.

## RESOURCES

Remind myself of the signs that a client has "forgotten" the limits of confidentiality.

Respond to those red flags by reopening the conversation to clarify the rules.

Review my informed consent forms to be sure they accurately represent my policies.

Make a list of circumstances when changes to confidentiality practices may occur in my own practice (e.g., changes in policy, changes in laws).

## DISCUSSION

Step 2 covers two informed consent conversations about confidentiality. First, at intake, you must give prospective clients enough information to allow them to make an informed decision about whether to confide in you in the first place. The second conversation comes at any time thereafter, whenever some change in circumstances increases the risk of disclosure, thus allowing the client to weigh the risks of confiding further. In either case, Step 2 deals with obtaining an informed client's consent to accept the limits of confidentiality that will apply to all clients, whereas obtaining client consent for voluntary client-specific disclosures are described in Step 3.

Both conversations share the same theoretical underpinnings. The importance of protecting the informed consent rights of mental health clients has long been well-documented in the professional literature (see, e.g., Appelbaum, Lidz, & Meisel, 1987; Barnett, Wise, Johnson-Greene, & Bucky, 2007; Beahrs & Gutheil, 2001; Beeman & Scott, 1991; Fisher, 2012, 2013; Haggerty & Hawkins, 2000; Handelsman, Kemper, Kesson-Craig, McLain, & Johnsrud, 1986; Hochhauser, 1999; Saks & Golshan, 2013; Somberg, Stone, & Claiborn, 1993).

The same ethical obligation underlies both conversations: Unless you intend to protect confidentiality unconditionally, you have an ethical obligation to inform clients about what the "conditions" will be (see Center for Ethical Practice, 2006). In most states, this is also a legal obligation: Licensing board regulations and state statutes can require mental health professionals to inform clients about the limits of confidentiality before rendering services.

Both conversations also raise similar clinical concerns:

> What does it mean to patients for a therapist to *begin* the relationship—or later to *interrupt* the clinical process—with a discussion of the fact that what the patient is about to confide may not remain confidential? Do such conversations inhibit patient self-disclosure (Nowell & Spruill, 1993) and limit the therapeutic outcome (Bollas & Sundelson, 1995), or do they create impressions of therapist trustworthiness and expertness (Sullivan, Martin, & Handelsman, 1993) and strengthen the therapeutic alliance (Joseph & Onek, 1999)? The research findings are mixed, but the answer seems to be "all of the above." Once informed about the limits of confidentiality, are therapy patients capable of wisely weighing the risk-benefit ratio of confiding their personal secrets to a therapist? Clinical opinions vary. (Fisher, 2013, p. 71)

Ethically speaking, however, such clinical concerns are completely irrelevant. Prospective clients have a right to know in advance what limits a therapist intends to place on confidentiality, so these conversations are ethically necessary regardless of their clinical impact. The only ethical way to avoid these informed consent conversations would be to decide to place no limits on confidentiality. As was noted in the Introduction, Step 2 is "optional" only for therapists brave enough to provide their clients with unconditional confidentiality, protecting information about their clients in all circumstances regardless of the risks to themselves. Most therapists avoid such risks to themselves by offering "conditional confidentiality" instead, but because this simply transfers the risk to clients, clients have the right to be informed about this risk before they consent to receive services.

Clear communication is important. To obtain "truly informed" consent from clients, the psychotherapist must clearly communicate the information they need for weighing the risks of confiding in the psychotherapist. Accuracy is also essential. Whether describing potential voluntary disclosures or explaining possible legally compelled disclosures, "whatever the clinician writes or says related to informed consent needs to be accurate" (Werth, Welfel, Benjamin, & Sales, 2009, p. 253). This is why the preparation in Step 1 was so important and why your consent forms should contain only accurate information about how you actually intend to behave (Pomerantz & Handelsman, 2004). Honesty is important because therapists' promises have serious consequences for clients. Therapists should use simple language to describe exactly how they intend to behave and should make only those promises which they are able and willing to keep (Fisher, 2013).

For this reason, as discussed in Step 1, no "canned" consent form will suffice at Step 2. You must personalize the form to describe what you will actually do and must write it in language that will be intelligible to the client. Also note that the Health Insurance Portability and Accountability Act of 1996 (HIPAA) "Notice of Privacy Practices" form is only an informational form, not a consent form. The client's signature simply acknowledges that the form was received. Finally, as described in the previous chapter, the HIPAA "Final Rule" (2013) now requires that "other uses and disclosures not described in the Privacy Notices will be made only with authorization from the individual" (HIPAA "Final Rule," 2013, p. 5623). In other words, before later making any disclosure not described to prospective clients here at Step 2 as a potential "limit of confidentiality," you are legally required to obtain the client's authorization at Step 3. This makes it important to plan this informed consent conversation carefully.

Mental health professionals who practice in group or agency settings may be required to use consent forms that have been prepared by others. However, these can be supplemented by oral discussion and, where allowed, they can also be supplemented by additional simplified information sheets or personalized forms (see Appendix D).

For minor clients, you can present the information in writing in age-appropriate language and then discuss it in detail, using examples of when you will keep secrets and when you will not. With adolescents, both the minor and the parents can be asked to provide consent in writing to accept your policies about confidentiality as a condition of receiving services (see sample adolescent informed consent form provided by Kraft, 2005).

Similarly, in couple or family therapy, the written description of your policies should include details about how you will handle information you receive from one participant when others are not present. For example, if one member of a couple phones you between sessions, will you always keep the content of that conversation a secret, will you always share it with the other member of the couple, or will you determine that on a case-by-case basis (Kuo, 2009; Weeks, Odell, & Methven, 2005)? Only if you determined such policy details in advance (Step 1) will you be prepared to explain your policies to both members of the couple in advance at intake (Step 2).

For group therapy clients, in addition to describing your own policies about confidentiality, you can stress the importance of participants protecting the confidentiality of other group members. You have the option of requiring that all group participants sign a statement promising to respect the confidentiality of the others. That statement can include an understanding that maintaining others' confidentiality is a condition of continuing to receive group services (Fisher, 2013; Knapp & VandeCreek, 2012). However, as required by the National Association of Social Workers (NASW) ethics code, psychotherapists "should inform participants in . . . group counseling that social workers cannot guarantee that all participants will honor such agreements" (NASW Ethical Standard 1.07(f), "Privacy and Confidentiality"). Research has suggested that group therapists tend to shortchange this conversation (Lasky & Riva, 2006; Roback, Moore, Bloch, & Shelton, 1996), but doing so can leave both clients and therapists vulnerable (Paradise & Kirby, 1990).

If third parties are paying for the psychotherapy or if the case was referred by an agency or ordered by a court, the conversation at Step 2 must include an explanation to the client about what information might be shared with the third party. Therapists can clarify this in advance: A contract with the third party can specify expectations about the sharing of client information and can sometimes place limits on the types of information that will be shared. The therapist is then in a position to assure that the prospective client(s) and all involved parties are clear about the potential limits of confidentiality.

The informed consent conversation at Step 2 should also include discussion of the confidentiality risks that arise from the use of technology in your practice setting. Recent professional ethics codes contain lists of technology-related items that clients should be informed about. For example, the American Counseling Association *ACA Code of Ethics and Standards of Practice* (2014) contains an entire section of Ethical Standards on "Distance Counseling, Technology, and Social Media."

Practice describing your policies about confidentiality out loud, until you can talk to prospective clients about the limits of confidentiality without sounding vague or defensive. (You can practice with anyone because your rules about confidentiality are not confidential.) Remember that the purpose of this conversation is to protect the client's right to know the rules in advance. Many therapists are reluctant to conduct these conversations or to provide enough information to fully inform clients. If you are among the reluctant ones, place yourself in the client's shoes and consider exactly when you would want your therapist to disclose the most private and confidential information about you without having informed you in advance about this risk.

Finally, this is a time to remember that your informed consent obligations go beyond the therapy client to include other parties that may be involved in the case. Asking, "Who is my client?" will lead to a singular answer, but in fact, our ethical obligations require us to think plurally instead (Fisher, 2009b, 2014). As described in the Step 1 chapter, The Trust (2006), a malpractice insurer, has provided an informed consent form to be used with "collaterals" who participate in others' therapy sessions without being the client.

> The professional has an obligation to clarify the ethical duties due each party, to inform all concerned about the ethical constraints, if any, and to take any steps necessary to ensure appropriate respect for the rights of the person at the bottom of the client hierarchy. (Koocher & Keith-Spiegel, 2008, p. 487)

## TAKING THE CLIENT'S PERSPECTIVE AT STEP 2: "UNINFORMED CONSENT" TO RECEIVE SERVICES

At the beginning of your first interview, your therapist asked you to sign some paperwork agreeing to receive services and agreeing to pay. You noticed that one of the papers mentioned *confidentiality*. When you asked the therapist what the rules are about that, his reply was, "There are some things I can't keep secrets about—like if you tell me about child abuse or say you are going to kill somebody—but the rest of the things on that page probably wouldn't apply to you."

This is an example of an inadequate informed consent conversation about the potential limits of confidentiality. If you were entering therapy yourself and were prepared to discuss your deepest feelings, dreams, fears, fantasies, and life experiences,

- Exactly which potential legal limitations on confidentiality would you want your potential therapist to "skip over" and not bother telling you about?
- Exactly which of this therapist's voluntary "nonconfidentiality policies" would you prefer to remain uninformed about?
- Exactly which other risks to your privacy might you consider too unlikely or too "unimportant" to be mentioned?

# Step 3. Obtain "Truly Informed" Consent Before Disclosing Confidential Information Voluntarily

Disclose Information Without Client Consent Only If Legally Unavoidable.

- ☐ Review Exhibit 1 (see "The Ethical ABCs of Conditional Confidentiality" chapter).
- ☐ Review my own practices to be sure I obtain consent for all my disclosures. (If consent for the disclosure was not obtained at intake, it must be obtained here.)
- ☐ Maintain current consent for disclosures made regularly; update signatures.
- ☐ Ensure that my consent forms indicate what will be disclosed and to whom.

http://dx.doi.org/10.1037/14860-005
*Confidentiality Limits in Psychotherapy: Ethics Checklists for Mental Health Professionals*, by M. A. Fisher

Inform Clients Adequately About the Nature and Implications of the Proposed Disclosure.

- ☐ Be explicit about which person(s) will receive the information I plan to disclose.
- ☐ Clearly describe the nature of the information I plan to disclose.
- ☐ Describe any foreseeable implications of disclosing or not disclosing it.
- ☐ Clarify whether the client wishes to deny consent for me to share certain information.

Obtain the Informed Client's Consent Before Disclosing Information; Document It in Writing.

- ☐ Have clients sign the "Release of Information Form" provided in Step 1.
- ☐ Fill in the nature of information and intended recipient.
- ☐ Fill in the expiration date before asking the client to sign.
- ☐ Review consent forms annually as a reminder to renew the consents that expire.

## RESOURCES

Except in emergencies, always obtain the client's consent in writing. Use the forms that were developed in Step 1, using Appendix E. For an expiration date, use the 1-year "rule of thumb," depending on the nature of services.

Use peer consultation and professional resources from previous chapters, as needed.

Allow ample time for discussion; do not shortcut the informed consent process.

## DISCUSSION

This chapter is about respecting the confidentiality rule. Its title emphasizes three concepts. First, the term *truly informed* is a reminder that, as described in the previous chapter, obtaining the client's informed consent to disclose information is a process that involves much more than obtaining a signature on a form. When we withhold from the client relevant information about what we will be disclosing or about the foreseeable implications of disclosing or not disclosing it, we are abridging the client's right to make an autonomous decision, and thus we are obtaining not truly informed consent but "coerced consent" or "uninformed consent" (Fisher, 2013, p. 75). Note that (a) consent is valid only if freely given and (b) consent is considered voluntarily given only if the client was first informed about the foreseeable implications of consenting. "Just because clients sign consent forms does not mean they understand the consequences of doing so. Our obligation is to teach clients about the broader principles that frame their requests for release of information" (VandeCreek, 2008, p. 373).

Second, the word *confidential* is a reminder that your obligations about confidentiality begin with your profession's confidentiality rule; every time you disclose client information you are making an exception to that rule.

> Respect for the obligation of confidentiality transcends the therapist's own judgment about whether or not the unauthorized release will be harmful to the patient. It is not the therapist's right to decide that an inappropriate disclosure is harmless just because he or she doesn't think the patient will suffer any adverse consequences. (Epstein, 1994, p. 182)

Therefore, before disclosing any information voluntarily, you must obtain the client's informed consent, either at intake, as described in the previous chapter (Step 2) or thereafter. "Because the patient holds the right to confidentiality, the therapist has an obligation to protect that right by making no voluntary exceptions to confidentiality without obtaining the patient's consent" (Fisher, 2013, p. 75). This chapter (Step 3) is about protecting the client's right to give "informed refusal" rather than give informed consent for information to be disclosed at any stage of the relationship.

Third, the term *voluntarily* helps distinguish between (a) the disclosures discussed in this chapter (Step 3), which therapists are legally free not to make and which clients can prevent by withholding consent and (b) the legally coerced disclosures (to be described in the next chapter, Step 4) that therapists are legally required to make "involuntarily" (i.e., even if they prefer not to and even if the client withholds consent). Note that "voluntary" and "involuntary" disclosures of confidential information are so different, ethically speaking, that they are discussed in separate chapters and defined separately in Appendix B.

The most frequent types of ethically appropriate voluntarily disclosures include those made to (a) other service providers (including the client's previous or current health care professionals, agencies that provide other services for the client, schools, etc.) or (b) family members who will be providing information about the client or who will be involved in the services provided.

The client who requests that the therapist share information or records with someone has a right to be informed about the content of what will be disclosed before giving consent for it to be shared. Therefore, a therapist who receives a "Consent for Release of Information" form that was obtained by someone else should not assume that the clients gave informed consent, because the other party could not have informed them about the nature of the information contained in the record that is about to be released. Informing clients before disclosing will protect their right to request that the therapist not disclose the information voluntarily or request that the therapist limit the information to be disclosed. "This need and this right are included in the meaning of *informed* in the term *informed consent*, and are based on respect for client autonomy and for people's rights and dignity." Through this process, clients can "gain an enhanced perspective on their right to keep personal information confidential" (VandeCreek, 2008, p. 373).

Decide whether to ask the client to provide (a) a one-way release (if you want only to obtain information from another person without disclosing any information yourself beyond identifying the client, as when requesting information from the client's former therapist) or (b) a two-way release (if you want to exchange information about the client with another party, either as an ongoing process, as with a current prescribing physician, or perhaps as a one-time exchange, as when acknowledging and clarifying a referral). Abbreviated samples of both types of "Consent for Release of Information" forms are provided in Appendix E.

The ethical rule of thumb is clear: Client consent should be obtained before any disclosures are made voluntarily. Even if the law allows you to disclose without obtaining client consent, it can be ethically important to do so. For example, ethically speaking, you should obtain consent to disclose information to the client's attorney, even though the attorney may advise you that, legally speaking, consent is not necessary. Similarly, the Health Insurance Portability and Accountability Act of 1996 does not legally require you to obtain consent before communicating with the client's other treating providers; however, as discussed in a later chapter ("Step 5. Avoid Preventable Breaches of Confidentiality"), our professions would ordinarily consider it ethically important to obtain consent for such communications.

The client's consent can be obtained either (a) by explaining at intake that this is an expected "limit of confidentiality" that all clients must accept as a condition of receiving services (Step 1) or (b) by later using a "Consent for Release of Information" form for client-specific disclosures (Step 3). As described earlier and illustrated in the vignette at the end of the chapter, it is important that this be informed consent, which requires informing the client about what will be disclosed before obtaining consent to disclose it.

Consent should be obtained in writing for disclosing client information during clinical supervision, as well as for obtaining peer consultation if any identifiable information will be disclosed. (For discussion of ethical distinctions between consultation and supervision, see Fisher, 2013, pp. 84–85.) For mental health professionals who engage in teaching or clinical writing, consent should be obtained if there will be any use of identifiable information about the client (Barnett, 2012; Fisher, 2013; Sieck, 2012; Woodhouse, 2012).

Perhaps Step 3 could be summarized this way: "Can you keep a secret? If you are a therapist, the correct answer is not just 'Yes, I can,' it is 'Yes,

I *must*,'" unless you have obtained consent from an informed client or are legally required to disclose (Fisher, 2013, p. 3). As always, it is important to take the client's perspective as a way of remembering the importance of informing the client about a disclosure and then obtaining consent from that informed client.

## TAKING THE CLIENT'S PERSPECTIVE AT STEP 3: "UNINFORMED CONSENT" TO DISCLOSE INFORMATION

You are the parent of a young child who recently began receiving therapy for anxiety, and you meet regularly with the child's therapist. She recommends that you make an appointment with a child psychiatrist to discuss the possible need for medication. She then asks you to sign forms giving consent for her to speak to the psychiatrist and to the child's teacher.

When you later meet with the psychiatrist and with the teacher, you discover that the therapist shared a great deal of your own personal, marital, family, and medical history that you did not expect her to disclose. You do not believe this information is relevant to the psychiatrist's work with your child, and you did not want this information shared with the school because it is your experience that information is not always treated as confidential in that setting.

When you confront the therapist, she simply reminds you that you signed a consent form saying that she could share "any and all information." You told her you did not realize this statement was on the form you signed, and you told her you would never have intended for her to share all the information she apparently disclosed. She merely stated that if you had wanted to place limits on what would be disclosed, it was your responsibility to say so.

Would you believe you were "truly informed" before you signed the consent form?

# Step 4. Respond Ethically to Laws That Require "Involuntary" Disclosures

Notify the Client of a Pending Legal Requirement to Disclose Information Without the Patient's Consent.

- ☐ Notify the client (or former client) if a legally required disclosure is pending.
- ☐ Empower the client—"pause" therapy to discuss the client's options for responding.
- ☐ Make exceptions only if the above would be clinically or legally inappropriate.

Respond Ethically to Legal Obligations (According to the Plan Provided in Step 1) for

- ☐ Laws requiring therapists to initiate disclosures (e.g., reporting laws)
- ☐ Laws granting others access to client information without client consent

http://dx.doi.org/10.1037/14860-006
*Confidentiality Limits in Psychotherapy: Ethics Checklists for Mental Health Professionals*, by M. A. Fisher

- ☐ Laws allowing recipients of information to redisclose without client consent
- ☐ Exceptions to therapist–client privilege in court cases

Limit Disclosure to the Extent Legally Possible.

- ☐ Understand my legal options and make use of protective laws when available.
- ☐ With the client's consent, consult with the client's attorney when appropriate.
- ☐ Use ethics consultants and legal consultants as needed.

If You Plan to Disobey Any Law That Requires You to Disclose Information,

- ☐ Learn the legal and/or financial penalty for the legal disobedience.
- ☐ Obtain consultation in advance about the implications.

## RESOURCES

Read the online article, "Protecting Confidentiality Rights" (Fisher, 2008); and

Chapter 7 ("Responding Ethically to Legal Demands for 'Involuntary' Disclosures of Patient Information") in *The Ethics of Conditional Confidentiality* (Fisher, 2013).

Study the response options in Appendix F for each law that can demand disclosure (see Appendix A for ethics texts and other relevant resources):

- How can I limit the amount of information I disclose?
- If a report is required, may I make it anonymously?
- If a report is required, may my client make it to protect our relationship?

## DISCUSSION

The previous chapter (Step 3) was about voluntary disclosures of confidential information that are made only if the client has given consent. This chapter (Step 4) is about a horse of a different color: *legally coerced* (i.e., "involuntary") disclosures. For a disclosure of confidential information to be considered voluntary, the client must have been free to withhold consent and the therapist must have been free not to disclose. In contrast, a disclosure is considered involuntary if it is legally required and therefore may need to be made without the client's consent and against the wishes of the therapist (Fisher, 2013).[1]

The legally required exceptions to confidentiality keep multiplying, and the possible ways of dealing with the exceptions have increased in complexity. It has been suggested that mental health professionals may be in danger of forgetting that these are exceptions and instead may be treating the exceptions as if they were the rule. "What occurs is a kind of *figure–ground reversal* [emphasis added]. When there are too many exceptions, the exceptions become prominent, and the rule fades into the background" (Beck, 1990, p. 5).

In an attempt to minimize such "figure–ground reversal," voluntary and involuntary disclosures are presented in this manual in two different chapters. From an ethical perspective, they represent two very different types of disclosures. They create different ethical obligations because their implications for clients are different. The problem is compounded by the fact that the legally required disclosures may not only publicly expose a client's problem (as in legally required abuse reports) but may also be unlimited in scope and may contain information that someone else wants to use against the client (as when courts order that client records or therapist testimony be used as evidence in a court case). Making such disclosures without client consent (or against a client's objections) would be deemed highly unethical if they were not legally required.

[1] Note that as used in this manual, the term *involuntary* is not synonymous with *unwilling*. It is a designation used for all legally required disclosures—even if you would have been willing to make that particular disclosure voluntarily—because, legally speaking, you have no choice (see the definitions in Appendix B).

Any discussion of legal details should evoke a recurring ethical refrain: A therapist's ethical responsibilities do not end where laws begin. "The mistake is to move from a premise that some action is legally required to a conclusion that it is ethically required. The unhappy truth is that ethical obligations can conflict with legal ones" (Kipnis, 2003, p. 1).

We have ethical and legal responsibility for protecting clients' confidentiality rights, and it is our recommendation that this include protecting their confidences to the extent allowed by law. How can you protect "confidentiality rights" when confidences are not legally protectable? You must first learn what the laws can require and then learn your legal options for responding ethically to the legal demands. Because laws can limit your ability to protect confidences, the confidentiality rights of today's therapy clients can be protected only through the following four-step approach, as reflected in the ethical practice model in Appendix G:

*Step 1: Prepare in advance by learning laws that can affect confidentiality.*

*Step 2: Inform prospective clients about potential legal limits of confidentiality* (thus protecting their right to protect themselves by withholding consent to treatment, or by limiting what they share, if they so choose).

*Step 3: Obtain consent from clients before disclosing information voluntarily* (allowing them to withhold consent for specific voluntary disclosures if they so choose).

*Step 4: Respond ethically to legal demands for involuntary disclosures* (to protect clients' confidences at least to the extent allowed by law).

Note what this involves: Unless you obtained the client's consent for a particular disclosure at intake (Step 2) or on a client-specific "Consent for Release of Information" form (Step 3), we advocate protecting confidentiality to the extent the law allows when a disclosure demand arises (Step 4).

This requires that we not think about the ethics of confidentiality merely in terms of obeying the minimum ethical and legal requirements, but instead think about the ethics of confidentiality in terms of the underlying moral principles. This is a "positive ethics" approach that allows us to engage in planful practices and prepare to take available legal initiatives to protect the confidentiality of clients who do not wish their information to be disclosed (Fisher, 2013). We recommend this out of respect for the confidences clients entrust to us and in protection of the rights and welfare of the clients who entrusted them.

Protecting confidentiality to the extent allowed by law is not a new idea. For those who think otherwise, it is important to recognize that this is actually a "mainstream" stance, respected by our professions, implied by (and in some cases advocated in) our professional ethics codes and guidelines, supported by the nondisclosure laws in each state, and affirmed by the U.S. Supreme Court in *Jaffee v. Redmond* (1996). The problem is that too often therapists are not clear about exactly what to do, so they may respond to legal requests or demands without contesting them.

This is not an extreme position. We could do much more, but the point here is simply that we should not do less. Some therapists have risked financial penalties and even risked incarceration by engaging in civil disobedience in the service of protecting client confidentiality when a court demanded disclosure and the client did not give consent (see, e.g., Beyer, 2000; Bollas & Sundelson, 1995; Kipnis, 2003). When legal requirements conflict with ethical responsibilities, the option of civil disobedience is included in a respected decision-making process for responding to the ethical–legal conflict (see Knapp, Gottlieb, Berman, & Handelsman, 2007). We are not advocating that therapists disobey the law, but that they should be willing to protect confidences at least to the extent the law allows. In today's legal climate, that can be challenging enough. Appendix F can be helpful in planning how to respond ethically to various types of legal demands.

This does require more than most ethics codes require, and it does require more than many therapists now do. Some clinicians, when faced with legal demands for client information, make no attempt to protect it or even to limit the scope of the disclosure. Sometimes they fail to protect the client's right to know in advance about the existence and the implications of their state's reporting laws or the possibility of subpoenas. Perhaps they are unaware of the laws or do not understand the available legal options for responding to them. Perhaps they are unaware of the ethical and legal implications of failing to use those legal options on the client's behalf. Perhaps they are victims of figure–ground confusion and equate legal demands with ethical requirements. Perhaps they are simply negligent. However, from the client's point of view, the result is the same regardless of the cause: Confidences are betrayed when they could have been protected.

Protecting confidentiality to the extent allowed by law may require some consultation before responding to the legal demand. Appendix F can be useful for assessing your knowledge of the laws in your own state and for determining which questions you should take to a legally informed colleague or to an attorney who is familiar with mental health law in your state. If you consult with an attorney, remember that although attorneys are experts about the law, you are responsible for being the expert about the ethics of your own profession.

For example, therapists who are unfamiliar with the exact requirements of their state's reporting laws should obtain consultation to determine the limits of what they are legally required to disclose and to whom. Otherwise, they may disclose unnecessarily, believing a report is legally required when it is not, and thereby may make unnecessary (and possibly unethical) disclosures. Research indicates that up to 75% of psychotherapists are misinformed about what is legally required in their own state regarding reports of danger to self and/or danger to others (Welfel, Werth, & Benjamin, 2009). Similarly, many are not familiar with the details of their state laws regarding the reporting of colleague misconduct, some of which do not require reporting if the disclosure would involve a breach of client confidentiality.

In court cases, therapists who are unfamiliar with court procedures may need consultation to be sure they do not confuse a subpoena with a court order. (For details about that distinction, see Appendix F, "Distinguishing Between Subpoenas and Court Orders" and "Responding Ethically to Subpoenas" sections.) A subpoena does not carry the same legal weight as a judge's order, and many ethical resources are available for planning how to respond protectively when you receive a subpoena (see, e.g., the discussion of subpoenas in American Psychological Association [APA] Committee on Legal Issues, 2006; APA Practice Organization, Legal and Regulatory Affairs Staff, 2008; Bennett et al., 2006; Childress-Beatty & Koocher, 2013; Fisher, 2012, 2013; Knapp & VandeCreek, 2012; Koocher & Keith-Spiegel, 2008; Pope & Vasquez, 2011; Younggren & Harris, 2008). Legal options vary from state to state; among the states for which state-specific recommendations are available online are Florida (Florida Psychological Association, n.d.), Pennsylvania (Baturin, Knapp, & Tepper, 2003), and Virginia (Fisher, 2007). The Step 6 chapter includes the suggestion that therapists can collaborate to create recommendations that fit the laws of their own state.

Even in the face of a court order, psychotherapists can sometimes limit disclosure. For example, the ethics code for counselors requires

> when ordered by a court to release confidential or privileged information without a client's permission, counselors seek to obtain written, informed consent from the client or take steps to prohibit the disclosure or have it limited as narrowly as possible because of potential harm to the client or counseling relationship. (American Counseling Association [ACA], 2014, Ethical Standard B.2.d, "Court-Ordered Disclosure")

The National Association of Social Workers (NASW) ethics code requires social workers to

> protect the confidentiality of clients during legal proceedings to the extent permitted by law. When a court of law or other legally authorized body orders social workers to disclose confidential or privileged information without a client's consent and such disclosure could cause harm to the client, social workers should request that the court withdraw the order or limit the order as narrowly as possible or maintain the records under seal, unavailable for public inspection. (NASW, 2008, Ethical Standard 1.07(j), "Privacy and Confidentiality")

The majority of mental health professionals have not obtained the specialized training required for doing forensic (i.e., court-related) work.

> Those who become involved simply because they feel the need to do the right thing, correct an injustice, or inappropriately advocate for a

> therapy patient do so at the risk of causing more problems than they solve. Despite the fact that these feelings are based on good intentions, they should be resisted; when they are, everyone benefits. (Gottlieb & Coleman, 2012, p. 119)

Finally, therapists who become involved in their clients' court cases must be aware of the potential for role confusion and the risks to clients if they multiply roles. Each court-related role can involve a different set of ethical obligations, which is why engaging in multiple roles (e.g., therapist plus evaluator or therapist plus expert witness) can create both ethical and legal complications. For this reason, professional ethics codes disallow certain role combinations.

For example, psychologists are prohibited from entering into any second role with their therapy client

> if the multiple relationship could reasonably be expected to impair the psychologist's objectivity, competence, or effectiveness in performing his or her functions as a psychologist, or otherwise risks exploitation or harm to the person with whom the professional relationship exists. (APA, 2010, Ethical Standard 3.05a)

and

> when psychologists are required by law, institutional policy, or extraordinary circumstances to serve in more than one role in judicial or administrative proceedings, at the outset they clarify role expectations and the extent of confidentiality and thereafter as changes occur. (APA, 2010, Ethical Standard 3.05c)

Similarly, forensic psychologists are advised:

> Providing forensic and therapeutic psychological services to the same individual or closely related individuals involves multiple relationships that may impair objectivity and/or cause exploitation or other harm. Therefore, when requested or ordered to provide either concurrent or sequential forensic and therapeutic services, forensic practitio-

> ners are encouraged to disclose the potential risk and make reasonable efforts to refer the request to another qualified provider. (APA, 2013, Guideline 4.02.01, "Therapeutic–Forensic Role Conflicts")

Counselors are similarly required to refrain from conducting court-related evaluations that involve conflicting roles: "Counselors do not evaluate current or former clients, clients' romantic partners, or clients' family members for forensic purposes. Counselors do not counsel individuals they are evaluating" (ACA, 2014, Ethical Standard A.6.d, "Role Changes in the Professional Relationship"). Marriage and family therapists are similarly required to avoid conflicting roles: "To avoid a conflict of interest, marriage and family therapists who treat minors or adults involved in custody or visitation actions may not also perform forensic evaluations for custody, residence, or visitation of the minor" (American Association for Marriage and Family Therapy, 2001, Ethical Standard 3.14, "Separation of Custody Evaluation From Therapy").

> Social workers who anticipate a conflict of interest among the individuals receiving services or who anticipate having to perform in potentially conflicting roles (for example, when a social worker is asked to testify in a child custody dispute or divorce proceedings involving clients) should clarify their role with the parties involved and take appropriate action to minimize any conflict of interest. (NASW, 2008, Ethical Standard 1.06(d)—"Conflicts of Interest")

Appendix F contains a chart describing the differential ethical responsibilities that apply in some of the voluntary and involuntary court-related roles undertaken by mental health professionals who have no formal forensic training. The next chapter (Step 5) contains further discussion of the importance of avoiding conflicting roles and inappropriate disclosures when participating voluntarily in a client's court case.

Being faced with a legal demand for disclosure can be anxiety provoking. The following vignette is a reminder of the importance of pausing to consider the client's perspective, and to be sure the client's interests are protected by limiting disclosures to the extent legally possible.

## TAKING THE CLIENT'S PERSPECTIVE AT STEP 4: THE CASE OF THE UNPROTECTIVE THERAPIST

Approximately one year after completing therapy, you decided to file for divorce and seek sole custody of your children. The attorney for your spouse, who is seeking sole custody himself on the grounds that he is a better parent, immediately sent a subpoena to your former therapist requesting your therapy records as evidence in the case. Without telling you, your former therapist immediately sent the records as requested. When subpoenaed to testify at the custody hearing, your former therapist complied without objection, and on the stand he answered questions in great detail, giving more information than necessary and reporting things you did not remember ever saying or doing.

You later discovered that the therapist should have contacted you first, so you could ask your attorney to file a motion to quash the subpoenas and protect the confidentiality of your therapy information. You confronted the therapist, who said he had never received a subpoena before and was not aware of exactly what to do about it. He said he was intimidated by it and thought it was a court order that he must obey immediately. As for his testimony, he said he felt badgered by your spouse's attorney and "couldn't think straight" on the stand.

Would you consider your former therapist's behavior to be adequately protective of your confidentiality rights?

# Step 5. Avoid Preventable Breaches of Confidentiality

Establish and Maintain Protective Policies and Procedures in an Office, Institution, or Agency.

- ☐ Write clear policies that describe the behavior I expect about confidentiality.
- ☐ If I transmit client information electronically, know HIPAA requirements:
  - ☐ Learn and enforce HIPAA Privacy Rule Requirements.
  - ☐ Learn and enforce HIPAA Security Rule Requirements.
  - ☐ Learn and enforce HIPAA Transaction Rule Requirements.
  - ☐ Learn and enforce HIPAA "Final Rule" Requirements.
- ☐ In all circumstances, disclose only the "minimum necessary" information.

http://dx.doi.org/10.1037/14860-007
*Confidentiality Limits in Psychotherapy: Ethics Checklists for Mental Health Professionals*, by M. A. Fisher

## RESOURCES

See Appendix C for a summary of HIPAA requirements, including workforce training requirements and the definition of "minimum necessary" disclosures.

Conduct Ethics-Based Staff Training About Confidentiality.

- ☐ Train all staff about professional ethical standards; provide ethics codes.
- ☐ Include clinical *and* nonclinical staff in ethics-based confidentiality training.
- ☐ Train clinical and nonclinical staff about record-keeping responsibilities.
- ☐ Review record-keeping practices regularly; enforce record security measures.
- ☐ Require everyone in the setting to sign a "confidentiality contract."

## RESOURCES

See Fisher (2009a) for an ethics-based training outline for clinical and nonclinical staff.

See Center for Ethical Practice (2009) for sample confidentiality contracts for staff.

See Center for Ethical Practice (2012) for a list of linked record keeping resources.

See References for articles and ethics texts that emphasize ethics of record keeping.

See the discussion that follows for other resources about record keeping and staff training.

Avoid "Informal" Discussions, "Unofficial" Disclosures, and Casual Conversations About Clients.

- ☐ Walk around my practice setting and *listen.* Do I hear client information?
- ☐ Walk around my practice setting and *look.* Do I see client information?
- ☐ Confirm that I have up-to-date consent for all conversations about clients.

## RESOURCES

Formalize and enforce all office policies that affect confidentiality.

Provide follow-up staff training to ensure that confidentiality will be protected.

Avoid Dual Roles That Can Create Conflicts of Interest in Courtroom and Elsewhere.

- ☐ Avoid unnecessary dual clinical roles with the same client.
- ☐ Do I wear more than one "hat" with the same client(s)?
- ☐ Does my combination of "hats" create confidentiality conflicts?
- ☐ Avoid voluntary nonclinical dual roles with clients when possible.
- ☐ Anticipate and try to avoid "involuntary" (i.e., legally imposed) dual roles or conflicts of interest (see also Step 4).

## RESOURCES

In Appendix A, see relevant ethics texts for resources about confidentiality conflicts in dual relationships.

Anticipate Legal Demands; Empower Clients to Act Protectively on Their Own Behalf.

- ☐ Learn all state laws that can demand or require me to disclose information.
- ☐ Anticipate circumstances when such laws might apply in each client's case.
- ☐ "Push the pause button" in therapy to inform clients about pending demands.
- ☐ Disclose the "minimum legally required" information unless the client has given consent for further disclosures.

## RESOURCES

See References for articles and books with information about ethical and legal issues. Review Step 4 and its Resources about responding to legal demands for disclosure.

Do Not Confuse Laws That *Permit* Me to Disclose With Laws That Legally *Require* Disclosure.

- ☐ Separate my list of laws into two categories: "permitting" or "requiring" disclosure (e.g., HIPAA permits many disclosures but requires none).
- ☐ Do not disclose in the "legally permitted" category without client consent.

## RESOURCES

See Appendix C for the distinction between "Laws Limiting Confidentiality" and "Laws Allowing Disclosure." Review the definition of "ethical ceiling" in Appendix B and review the discussion of that concept in the Introduction and elsewhere. See Step 1 and renew legal resources as appropriate. Review Appendix B for definitions of legal terms related to confidentiality

In the chapter, "The Ethical ABCs of Conditional Confidentiality," see Exhibit 1, "Protecting Clients' Confidentiality Rights: An Ethical Practice Model" and accompanying text.

## DISCUSSION

Step 5 is a reminder that most behavior about confidentiality still remains entirely within the psychotherapist's control (Fisher, 2008). As used here, the term *preventable* refers to voluntary disclosures that are made without obtaining the required consent and in the absence of any of the legal requirements discussed in Step 4.

> This includes informal disclosures to colleagues; gossip to family or friends; conversations about patients in social settings; appropriate conversations in inappropriate places (e.g., peer consultations in hallways or public restaurants); potentially appropriate disclosures without appropriate consent (e.g., disclosing sensitive personal information to a prescribing physician without explicit patient consent); overdisclosures (e.g., disclosing beyond what the patient authorized, or beyond what is needed in the circumstance); disclosures triggered by "technology glitches"; and so forth. Such breaches are avoidable. They place clients at risk and thereby place psychologists at risk. (Fisher, 2008, p. 11)

Psychotherapists are not ethically free to disclose client information without client consent simply because they convince themselves that the client will not likely be harmed by that particular breach of confidentiality.

> When patients discover that information has been released without authorization, they often feel as if a piece of themselves has been misappropriated. By maintaining a patient's confidence, a therapist transmits a defining behavioral message that is trust-enhancing and ego strengthening. (Epstein, 1994, p. 182)

> In our experience, most mental health professionals are by nature and training concerned about confidentiality. Usually, they do not knowingly and intentionally share confidential client information with other individuals. Yet breaches of confidentiality seem to occur relatively frequently and can easily result in potential harm to a client and a complaint against one's license. We believe that many such breaches are caused by a combination of factors, including but not limited to poor attention to detail, the absence of or failure to follow routine policies and procedures, a loss of focus on one's own behavior as it relates to maintaining confidentiality, and behaving with good intentions but in a way that falls outside of accepted standards of care. (Barnett, Zimmerman, & Walfish, 2014, p. 71)

Within the clinical setting, psychotherapists have ethical responsibilities about confidentiality that extend beyond their own behavior. Knapp and VandeCreek (2012) advocated the fostering of a "culture of safety" in which protection of clients' rights becomes everyone's responsibility (p. 187). This can include devising protective policies and procedures about privacy and confidentiality and expecting them to be followed by all staff, both clinical and nonclinical.

Staff training is important for preventing "accidental" disclosures, which Knapp (2002) defined as "unintended lapses or unanticipated problems" (p. 6). Staff carelessness in transmitting client information electronically, including accidental misdials on the fax machine and errors in e-mail addresses, can send confidential information to the wrong destination. Oversights, such as unattended computers or failure to institute password protections, can place all client data at risk. Similarly, allowing staff members to remove client data from the clinical setting can result in lost disks or stolen laptops that could undo the confidentiality of many clients at once.[1] Such risks, and their implications, should be discussed in

[1] Note that in some states, in addition to the ethical issues involved, it is illegal for staff to remove client information from the workplace without the explicit consent of the person who owns the records (see, e.g., Virginia § 32.1-127.1:02).

formal ethics-based confidentiality training that is attended by all staff (Fisher, 2013).

"Workforce training" is legally required by the federal Health Insurance Portability and Accountability Act of 1996 (HIPAA; see the summary in Appendix C). The ethical practice model presented in this manual can be useful for creating ethics-based confidentiality training to supplement the legal-based HIPAA training that staff might have already obtained elsewhere (Fisher, 2009a). All staff, both clinical and nonclinical, can be required to sign confidentiality agreements as a condition of employment. Such contracts can include requirements about ensuring the safety of client records stored in hardcopy, as well as requirements about the safety of confidential information stored or transmitted using electronic technology (see sample confidentiality contracts at Center for Ethical Practice, 2009).

Misunderstandings about laws can lead to unnecessary and easily avoidable breaches of confidentiality. For example, some reporting laws apply only in certain circumstances or with certain populations, and misinterpreting such laws can lead you to breach confidentiality unnecessarily. Step 1, "Preparation," was the place to clarify what is legally required by each of the laws in your state that place limits on your ability to protect confidentiality. Step 4 and Appendix D cover recommendations about responding ethically to legal demands.

Role confusion can also lead to preventable confidentiality conflicts and inappropriate disclosures. These can arise if you are unclear about the ethical implications of a particular role or if you multiply roles (i.e., wear more than one "hat" with the same person). Ethical conflicts about confidentiality arise in any case when you take on two different roles that create two different sets of ethical obligations about confidentiality.

As noted in Step 4, it can be especially important to be alert for role confusion when accepting voluntary court-related roles that would require you to don a second hat atop an existing therapist hat. For example, in your role as psychotherapist, you are ethically required to protect the confidentiality of your therapy client, but if you then agree to conduct a court-ordered psychological evaluation for that same therapy client, that second role demands that you disclose information to the court. You would be required to inform the client that the information obtained in that evaluation would be made available to the court, but in practical terms, it can turn out to be impossible to separate the confidential information learned during the therapy process from the information learned during the court-related evaluation. For this reason, formal forensic evaluation roles should not be voluntarily undertaken with individuals for whom you are (or have previously been) in the role of psychotherapist (see American Psychological Association [APA], 2013; Center for Ethical Practice, 2014b).

When a therapist accepts a court-related role at the request of a client, it is important to obtain the client's informed consent. This requires that the therapist first inform the client about the implications of taking on that role. For example, before obtaining the client's consent to release records, inform the client about exactly what is contained in the records; and before obtaining the client's consent to provide testimony in a court case voluntarily (i.e., at the client's request and in the absence of a court order), inform the client about the types of questions that might be asked, give some examples, and explain the answers that you might give. The chart, "Which Hat Are You Wearing" in Appendix F provides brief summaries of the differential confidentiality and informed consent obligations in several court-related roles that therapists might enter voluntarily.

In couple or family cases, it is important that everyone understand your rules about information one person confides when others are not present (e.g., you can explain whether the content of phone calls from one person will be disclosed to others). Multiparty cases can also create confidentiality dilemmas if you have failed to inform all involved parties in advance (Step 2) about the confidentiality implications of their participation (Fisher, 2009b). For example, when parents are seen as "collaterals" to their child's therapy or family members are seen as collaterals in an adult therapy case, they must be informed that this role may give them fewer confidentiality rights than will be afforded to the therapy client. This becomes especially important if custody situations arise and parents were not informed of the limits to their rights (see sample Collateral Consent Form at The Trust, 2006.) In advance, it is also important to clarify with all prospective parties the understandings you have reached with referral agencies who may be paying for the services and who may desire to receive regular reports of client attendance or progress.

Step 5 can also serve as a reminder that the onset of managed care created no new ethically permitted exceptions to the rule of confidentiality. If you have signed third-party provider contracts, it is important to review them carefully to understand the circumstances when you have thereby entered into a legal agreement to disclose client information. You must be prepared to explain that limitation on confidentiality to prospective clients (see, e.g., APA Practice Organization Legal and Regulatory Affairs Staff, 2005a, 2005b; Cooper & Gottlieb, 2000; Davidson & Davidson, 1996; Koman & Harris, 2005).

Psychotherapists sometimes treat disclosures for third-party reimbursement as if they were "involuntary" because they feel "financially coerced" to disclose certain information. The "figure–ground reversal" (Beck, 1990) described in Step 4 is common in this area of practice, and it occurs when disclosures without informed consent become the rule rather than the exception. The HIPAA regulations do legally allow disclosures for reimbursement purposes without the client's explicit consent, but ethically speaking, these are voluntary disclosures, so they do have to be discussed in the initial informed consent conversation (Step 2). Because it is impossible at intake to predict the content of future disclosures, the "usual rule of thumb" should be to also discuss treatment plans and other disclosed information at the time of transmission (Acuff et al., 1999, p. 570) and to obtain explicit consent for disclosure of that particular information at Step 3 (VandeCreek, 2008).

Advances in technology have compounded the problem. In submitting claims for reimbursement, clinicians and their office staff have become dangerously accustomed to initiating routine electronic transmission of private and sensitive information, often without adequately informing clients of the content or discussing the implications of the disclosure and sometimes without obtaining client consent at all (Fisher, 2013).

Some of the problems that fall under Step 5 can be easily remedied. Others, however, can take extensive planning and careful execution, including staff training and cooperative enforcement. This is a good opportunity to return to Step 1, "Preparation," and review whether your advance planning was complete and to initiate training of both clinical and nonclinical staff in your setting and consult with and collaborate with colleagues in clarifying policies and procedures that might affect confidentiality, as suggested in Step 6.

Finally, regardless of the context, Step 5, "Avoiding Preventable Disclosures," is a reminder that it is ethically and legally important to release only the minimum amount of information necessary for the purpose. Ethically, the importance of this is reflected in therapists' professional ethics codes: For counselors, "when circumstances require the disclosure of confidential information, only essential information is revealed" (American Counseling Association, 2014, Ethical Standard B.2.e, "Minimal Disclosure"), psychiatrists "may disclose only that information which is relevant to a given situation" (American Psychiatric Association, 2009, Ethical Standard 4 (5)), psychologists "include in written and oral reports and consultations only information germane to the purpose for which the communication is made" (APA, 2010, Ethical Standard 4.04, "Minimizing Intrusions on Privacy"), and social workers "should disclose the least amount of confidential information necessary to achieve the desired purpose; only information that is directly relevant to the purpose for which the disclosure is made should be revealed" (National Association of Social Workers, 2008, Ethical Standard 1.07(c), "Privacy and Confidentiality"). Legally, the federal HIPAA regulations mirror these requirements (see Appendix C for the HIPAA definition of "minimum necessary" disclosure of confidential client information).

The following vignette illustrates some of the problems that can result when the psychotherapist does not prevent "avoidable" disclosures of confidential client information.

## TAKING THE CLIENT'S PERSPECTIVE AT STEP 5: THE CASE OF THE AVOIDABLE DISCLOSURES

You have been meeting with a therapist for the past 6 weeks, but you have begun to think you made a bad choice. You list the problems:

First, the setting itself does not seem conducive to confidential relationships. In the elevator, a secretary was talking to someone about the client your therapist had just seen. At the check-in window, you could see the clerk's computer screen with other clients' names on it, and the sign-in sheet had previous clients' signatures on it. Sitting in the waiting room, you could hear some clients' voices from nearby therapy rooms, and you could hear the accountant down the hall complaining that Mr. Jones did not pay his bill.

Second, your therapist does not ever seem to give you a straight answer about anything. When you asked hypothetical questions such as, "If I told you about ________, could you keep that a secret?," you received an exploration of your concerns about confidentiality rather than a "yes" or "no" answer about how he would actually behave. Your therapist has also never told you whether his colleagues in the same practice group have access to your records.

Third, you have discovered that your therapist attends the weekly poker game in which your son also participates. At their last game, he told your son he knew you. According to your son, they are considering a business deal together, but the therapist has never mentioned any of this to you, and you worry that this creates a conflict of interest for him.

Perhaps it is no surprise that you are considering a change of therapists.

# Step 6. Talk About Confidentiality: Educate Each Other and the Public

Go Public: Refuse to Keep Confidentiality Problems a Secret.

- ☐ Find ways to discuss confidentiality issues safely and ethically with others.
- ☐ Be willing to raise the general issues with colleagues and in public settings.

Model Ethical Practices: Confront Others' Unethical Practices.

- ☐ Practice ethically and explain the ethical basis for my decisions.
- ☐ Call others' attention to unethical confidentiality practices; offer resources.

http://dx.doi.org/10.1037/14860-008
*Confidentiality Limits in Psychotherapy: Ethics Checklists for Mental Health Professionals*, by M. A. Fisher

Teach Ethical Practices to Employees, Students, Supervisees, and Agency Administrators.

- ☐ Provide the ethical practice model (see Exhibit 1) to students and supervisees.
- ☐ Use the ethical practice model for training clinical and nonclinical staff.
- ☐ Provide legal updates to staff and trainees as refreshers or if laws change.

Educate Attorneys, Judges, and the Public About the Importance of Confidentiality in Therapy.

- ☐ In court cases, explain how confidentiality ethics varies, depending on my role.
- ☐ Respond ethically to subpoenas; protect confidentiality to the extent legally possible.

Explore Possibilities for Legislative Change Toward More Protective Confidentiality Laws.

- ☐ Join others in lobbying for client-protective legislative changes when needed.
- ☐ Encourage state professional associations to monitor for new legal incursions.

Develop Multidisciplinary Training, Continuing Education, and Consultation.

- ☐ Share the ethical practice model with peers and consultation groups.
- ☐ Create multidisciplinary, ethics-based continuing education workshops about confidentiality.

## RESOURCES

See Table F.1 in Appendix F, "Which Hat Are You Wearing? Differential Ethical Obligations in Voluntary and Involuntary Court-Related Roles."

See Fisher (2008), "Protecting Confidentiality Rights: The Need for an Ethical Practice Model"; Fisher (2009a), "Ethics-Based Training for Non-Clinical Staff in Mental Health Settings"; Fisher (2013) "The Ethics of Conditional Confidentiality: A Practice Model for Mental Health Professionals" (Chapter 9).

## DISCUSSION

This is the final step in the ethical practice model. The focus here is on providing ongoing education, consultation, and support to each other; collaborating about this aspect of practice; and joining in broader actions toward improving confidentiality protections. This requires that we create conversations about confidentiality, both with each other and with others.

When therapists fail to consult with others and allow themselves to become overly anxious about confidentiality, they are at risk of creating self-imposed isolation and a great deal of secrecy about their confidentiality dilemmas. Yet, what therapists need is the opposite—more open conversations with colleagues about their problems in maintaining clients' confidences, more mutual understanding of the difficult legal and financial decisions that they all face about this aspect of clinical practice, and more opportunities to learn from each others' successes and failures. When therapists stop hiding their confidentiality problems, they can be less fearful of being "discovered," more willing to ask for help in advance, better able to predict and avoid self-inflicted ethical dilemmas, and more likely to learn from past mistakes, both their own and those of others (Fisher, 2013).

When psychotherapists hide their confidentiality problems and remain fearful that they will be discovered, they lose the opportunity to learn from each other's successes and mistakes, and they fail to ask for help in advance. This leaves them less able to predict and avoid self-inflicted ethical dilemmas and unlikely to learn enough from past mistakes, whether their own or those of others.

Psychotherapists' policies about confidentiality are not confidential. Their confidentiality dilemmas can be talked about as long as clients are not identified.

> First, therapists need to acknowledge that the issue exists. Is confidentiality important? If it is, then it's worth defending. . . . Before anything, they can *talk* about the issue. The changes we describe in our book happened at least in part because the profession was asleep at the wheel. Now it needs to wake up and look the crisis in the face. (Bollas & Langs, 1999, p. 1)

For starters, as suggested at the beginning of this manual, consider tackling this manual as a group project. Forming a peer group for that purpose can be a way of meeting new colleagues, introducing them to confidentiality issues, pooling resources, and sharing the planning. Such a group can also be an ongoing and reliable source of good consultation and support when facing difficult confidentiality dilemmas. It has been suggested that "creating ways to stay in connection with others seems to be one of the most basic, important, and helpful self-care strategies" for many psychotherapists (Pope & Vasquez, 2005, p. 16), and this project can create important connections with colleagues.

The ethical practice model can be a shared language for creating clearer conversations about this complex and difficult aspect of practice (Fisher, 2008, 2012, 2013). It can be helpful not only in consultations with colleagues but also when training and supervising students about confidentiality, when teaching staff and employees in clinical settings, and when writing about confidentiality responsibilities in academic and clinical journals. In broader public contexts, the model can be the basis for educating attorneys, judges, legislators, and the public. Finally, it can be useful in helping others understand the need for legislative reform in situations where laws conflict with clinical confidentiality.

> If we, as a profession and as individual practitioners, are to address the possible conflicts between the law and the welfare of our patients, one of the initial steps is to engage in frequent, open, and honest discussion of the issue. The topic must be addressed in our graduate courses, internship programs, case conferences, professional conventions, and informal discussions with our colleagues. (Pope & Vasquez, 2011, p. 89)

Because complications about therapeutic confidentiality span all professions and settings, conversations about it can create cooperation across professional lines. This can include such things as group consultation for creating and providing staff training about confidentiality (Fisher, 2009a), as well as individual consultation when particular clinical roles create dilemmas about confidentiality (Center for Ethical Practice, 2014b). This can also include working together to create collaborative consultation networks at the local level, as well as multidisciplinary training and continuing education at the state level (Fisher, 2012). Because ethical decisions are often influenced by nonrational processes (Rogerson, Gottlieb, Handelsman, Knapp, & Younggren, 2011), collaboration can be helpful in monitoring and maintaining objectivity in our own decision making.

Conversations about confidentiality can take many different forms. For conversations among colleagues, consider exploring some or all of the following possibilities:

- Create conversations with other psychotherapists toward goals such as self-understanding, policy planning, and support about difficult confidentiality issues.
- Initiate individual or group conversations with colleagues to tackle complicated ethical and legal questions as "hypotheticals" in advance of a dilemma or crisis.
- Consult with colleagues in the process of creating and editing your client handouts and other written materials about confidentiality.
- Join with colleagues to plan and provide ethics-based training and legal updates for nonclinical staff in your mental health settings.

Conversations about confidentiality can include interdisciplinary cooperation and collaboration. This manual is an example of the fact that the basic rules about confidentiality apply to all disciplines, and we can all learn from each other's ethics codes. The possibilities include efforts such as the following:

- Plan joint local or state-wide training about confidentiality that includes mental health service providers of all professions.
- Schedule joint legal updates when there are changes in state laws that affect the confidentiality of all psychotherapy clients.

Finally, conversations about confidentiality can be part of wider goals that include public education and legislative reform.

- Plan individual or group conversations to educate potential consumers about what to expect about confidentiality in psychotherapy.
- Engage in individual conversations or group education for attorneys, judges, and other court personnel to clarify any misunderstandings about the differential ethical implications of the various roles mental health professionals can play in court cases.
- Consider joining with colleagues to lobby for improved legal protections of confidentiality in your state.

The following vignette is a reminder of the potential harms that can result when psychotherapists become isolated in ways that leave clients' rights unprotected.

## TAKING THE CLIENT'S PERSPECTIVE AT STEP 6: THE CASE OF THE "DISCONNECTED" THERAPIST

You just finished meeting for the first time with a prospective therapist. He belongs to a highly regarded group practice, but he did not seem familiar with state laws that affect confidentiality or even knowledgeable about the consent forms that are used by his own practice group. At intake, when he presented you with the group's informed consent form, he said he thought the form was unintelligible, but that your signature was required. He was unable to answer questions about some of the stated policies about confidentiality.

When you asked whether he spends time discussing such matters with his colleagues in the practice group or attending professional training sessions about such things, he replied that he prefers to spend time helping clients, not discussing laws with colleagues and "designing more paperwork" for the group practice.

He has the reputation of being a good clinician, so you are trying to decide whether to work with him anyway, even though he seems unable to provide clear answers about exactly when he will keep secrets and when he will not. You are concerned that he seems disconnected from his professional colleagues and his profession's ethical standards.

Will you choose this therapist?

# Appendix A: Online Sources for Professional Ethics Codes and Listing of Ethics Texts

The following are links to ethics codes of major mental health professions, followed by links to ethical guidelines for some of the subspecialties within these fields. Active links for this list are available at http://www.centerforethicalpractice.org/ethical-legal-resources/ethical-information/ethics-codes.

## COUNSELORS

American Counseling Association Code of Ethics (2014): http://www.counseling.org/docs/ethics/2014-aca-code-of-ethics.pdf?sfvrsn=4

National Board for Certified Counselors Code of Ethics (2012): http://www.nbcc.org/Assets/Ethics/NBCCCodeofEthics.pdf

## NURSES

American Nurses Association Code of Ethics For Nurses With Interpretive Statements (2015): http://www.nursingworld.org/MainMenuCategories/EthicsStandards/CodeofEthicsforNurses

## PSYCHIATRISTS

Principles of Medical Ethics With Annotations Especially Applicable to Psychiatry (2013): http://www.psychiatry.org/practice/ethics/resources-standards

## PSYCHOLOLOGISTS

American Psychological Association (APA) Ethical Principles of Psychologists and Code of Conduct (2010): http://www.apa.org/ethics/code/index.aspx

## SOCIAL WORKERS

Clinical Social Work Association Code of Ethics (1997; reviewed 2006): http://associationsites.com/CSWA/collection/Ethcs%20Code%20Locked%2006.pdf

Code of Ethics of the National Association of Social Workers (2008): http://www.socialworkers.org/pubs/code/code.asp

## SUBSPECIALTIES WITHIN THESE FIELDS: ETHICS CODES AND PROFESSIONAL GUIDELINES

Employee Assistance Programs (EAPs): Ethical Framework for the Use of Technology in EAPs (2011)
http://onlinetherapyinstitute.com/ethical-framework-for-the-use-of-technology-in-eaps/

Forensic Psychiatrists: American Academy of Psychiatry and the Law Ethics Guidelines for Practice of Forensic Psychiatry (2005)
http://www.aapl.org/ethics.htm

Forensic Psychologists: Specialty Guidelines for Forensic Psychology (2013)
https://www.apa.org/practice/guidelines/forensic-psychology.aspx

Forensic Training (All Professions): Association of Family and Conciliation Courts (Resources; 2015)
http://www.afccnet.org/

Group Therapists: AGPA (American Group Psychotherapy Association) and IBCGP (International Board for Certification of Group Psychotherapists) Guidelines for Ethics (2002)
http://www.agpa.org/home/practice-resources/ethics-in-group-therapy

Interpreters for the Deaf: National Association of the Deaf and Registry of Interpreters of the Deaf Code of Professional Conduct (2005)
http://www.rid.org/ethics/code-of-professional-conduct/

Pastoral Counselors: American Association of Pastoral Counselors Code of Ethics (2012)
http://www.aapc.org/Default.aspx?ssid=74&NavPTypeId=1161

Psychoanalysts: American Psychoanalytic Association Principles and Standards of Ethics for Psychoanalysts (2008)
http://www.apsa.org/code-of-ethics

Psychologists: Links to APA Resources Online (2015)
http://www.centerforethicalpractice.org/Links-Psychologists.htm

Psychologists (Clinical and School): Code of Fair Testing Practices in Education (APA, 2004)
http://www.apa.org/science/programs/testing/fair-code.aspx

School Psychologists: National Association of School Psychologists Principles for Professional Ethics (2010)
http://www.nasponline.org/assets/Documents/Standards%20and%20Certification/Standards/1_%20Ethical%20Principles.pdf

Substance Abuse: NAADAC (National Association of Alcohol and Drug Abuse Counselors), the Association of Addiction Professionals Code of Ethics (n.d.)
http://www.naadac.org/code-of-ethics

## ETHICS TEXTS

Anderson, S. K., & Handelsman, M. M. (2010). *Ethics for psychotherapists and counselors: A proactive approach.* Malden, MA: Wiley-Blackwell.

Barnett, J. E., & Johnson, W. B. (2010). *Ethics desk reference for counselors.* Alexandria, VA: American Counseling Association.

Haas, L. J., & Malouf, J. L. (2005). *Keeping up the good work: A practitioner's guide to mental health ethics* (4th ed.). Sarasota, FL: Professional Resource Press.

Jacob, S., Decker, D. M., & Hartshorne, T. S. (2010). *Ethics and law for school psychologists* (6th ed.). Hoboken NJ: Wiley.

Knapp, S. J., & VandeCreek, L. D. (2012). *Practical ethics for psychologists: A positive approach* (2nd ed.). Washington, DC: American Psychological Association.

Koocher, G. P., & Keith-Spiegel, P. (2008). *Ethics in psychology and the mental health professions: Standards and cases* (3rd ed.). New York, NY: Oxford University Press.

Pope, K. S., & Vasquez, M. J. T. (2011). *Ethics in psychotherapy and counseling: A practical guide* (4th ed.). Hoboken, NJ: Wiley. http://dx.doi.org/10.1002/9781118001875

Reamer, F. G. (2009). *The social work ethics casebook.* Washington, DC: NASW Press.

# Appendix B: Definitions and Clarifications

## TERMS ABOUT CONFIDENTIALITY

*Confidentiality rights*: The client's rights regarding confidentiality of information, as stipulated in the ethics codes of mental health professionals and/or by law.

*Absolute confidentiality*: Confidentiality is maintained without exception, with disclosure of no information unless the client has given informed consent.

*Conditional confidentiality*: Confidentiality is maintained, but certain exceptions or "conditions" are imposed.

## PERSPECTIVES ABOUT PROFESSIONAL BEHAVIOR

*Ethical focus*: Attention to the practices that are most protective of clients and their rights. (This includes following the ethical standards described in one's professional ethics code. It can also include attention to one's own personal ethical values that might create supererogatory standards beyond those minimum standards.)

*Legal focus*: Attention to what one's laws and regulations might require, permit, or prohibit.

---

*Risk-management focus*: Attention on minimizing the legal risks to oneself (e.g., identifying ways in which clients can be harmed—or perceive themselves to be harmed—for the purpose of protecting oneself from allegations of misconduct, whether founded or frivolous). (Knapp & VandeCreek, 2012, p. 11.)

## TERMS DESCRIBING ETHICAL BEHAVIOR

*Ethically required*: Behavior explicitly required by a professional ethics code (e.g., therapists must inform prospective clients about the limits of confidentiality before providing services).

*Ethically allowed or ethically permitted*: Behavior explicitly allowed (but not required) by an ethics code (e.g., therapists are ethically free to disclose confidential information in certain specific circumstances).

*Ethically prohibited*: Behavior explicitly disallowed by an ethics code (e.g., therapists may not audio tape clients without their consent; therapists are ethically prohibited from engaging in sexual relationships with current clients).

"*Ethical floor*": A standard of behavior that complies with the letter of the ethics code (i.e., the minimum standards required by the profession).

"*Ethical ceiling*": A voluntary standard of behavior that is even more client protective than the ethics code requires (e.g., following personally imposed supererogatory standards such as never disclosing anything without a client's informed consent unless legally required to do so; not disclosing information simply because some law allows it).

## TERMS DESCRIBING DIFFERENTIAL LEGAL CIRCUMSTANCES

*Legally required*: Behavior that is explicitly mandated by state or federal statute, regulation, or case law (e.g., most states have laws that legally require therapists to report child abuse).

*Legally allowed or legally permitted*: Behavior that is allowed (but not required) by law or regulation (e.g., HIPAA legally permits—but does not legally require—disclosure of client information without specific client authorization for certain treatment, payment, or health care operations).

*Legally prohibited*: Behavior that is explicitly disallowed by some law or regulation (e.g., most state licensing boards legally prohibit therapists from engaging in sexual relationships with current clients).

## TERMS DESCRIBING TYPES OF DISCLOSURES OF CONFIDENTIAL INFORMATION

*Voluntary disclosures*: Disclosures of identifiable client information that are not legally required (meaning that therapists would be free not to disclose and clients are free not to give consent for them to disclose).

*"Involuntary" disclosures*: Disclosures of confidential information that are required by law (meaning that therapists are legally required to disclose in that circumstance whether or not they or the client wants the information to be released). In other words, as used in this manual, the term *involuntary* is not synonymous with *unwilling*. The term *involuntary disclosure* is used whenever the therapist has no legal choice but to disclose, even if the therapist would have been willing to make that disclosure voluntarily.

## DISTINGUISHING AMONG PRIVACY, CONFIDENTIALITY, AND PRIVILEGE

Figure B.1 represents the relationship among the terms *privacy*, *confidentiality*, and *privilege*. Some people use these terms interchangeably, as if they were synonymous, but they are not. They are interrelated, but their differences are important.

*Privacy* is a broad concept related to protection from others. The right to privacy is the right to be protected from visibility, access, or intrusion by others—the right not to be public. For example, mental health professionals can enhance privacy by creating office arrangements that allow clients to enter and leave by doors not visible to others, by preventing others from

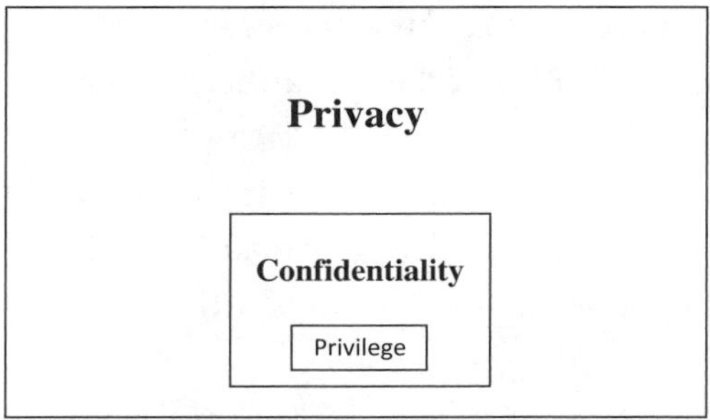


**Figure B.1**

Distinguishing among privacy, confidentiality, and privilege. From "'What Should I Do?'—39 Ethical Dilemmas Involving Confidentiality," by G. P. Koocher and P. Keith-Spiegel, 2009, retrieved from http://www.continuingedcourses.net/active/courses/course049.php. Copyright 2009 by G. P. Koocher and P. Keith-Spiegel. Adapted with permission.

entering if a therapy session is in process, by establishing sound barriers to prevent voices from being heard outside the room, and so forth.

*Confidentiality* is a subcategory of privacy that involves informational privacy. The right to confidentiality is the right to prevent information about oneself from being made available to others. Mental health professionals have an ethical duty to protect this right. The client's right to confidentiality of the information obtained and held by a mental health professional is protected both ethically (by the ethics code of each profession) and legally (by state and federal nondisclosure laws).

*Privilege* is a subcategory of confidentiality that applies only in legal contexts. State and federal laws can grant "privileged" status to certain relationships (e.g., husband–wife, attorney–client, priest–penitent, doctor–client), meaning that the information communicated within that relationship is legally protected from being used as evidence in a court case. State laws vary in the extent to which information from the therapist–client relationship is "privileged," and they vary in their exceptions to privilege that allow judges to order a psychotherapist to make client information available as evidence in state court cases. In federal court cases, privilege is governed by Rule 501 of the Federal Rules of Evidence.

# Appendix C: Laws and Regulations Affecting Confidentiality

## TYPES OF LAWS AFFECTING CONFIDENTIALITY[1]

### Laws Protecting Confidentiality

There are two types of laws that can help psychotherapists protect confidentiality, one of which applies only in court cases.

#### *Nondisclosure Laws or "Confidentiality Laws"*

These laws are the legal equivalent of the ethical confidentiality rule—they impose a legal duty to protect the confidentiality of psychotherapy clients. These laws prevent psychotherapists from voluntarily disclosing confidential information without the client's consent. At the state level, these include nondisclosure statutes and regulations, including licensing board regulations. At the federal level, they include the statutes and regulations providing special protections in cases involving federally funded substance abuse treatment, as well as the nondisclosure rules and confidentiality protections in the Health Insurance Portability and Accountability Act of 1996 (HIPAA) regulations (discussed later).

[1] For examples of each type of law, see the Center for Ethical Practice website (http://www.centerforethicalpractice.org/lawsaffectingconfidentiality).

### *Privilege Laws*

Every state has one or more statutes granting the therapist–client relationship the status of *privileged relationship*, meaning that communications from that relationship are protected from being used as evidence in a court case. The exceptions to privilege vary significantly from state to state. No state's privilege laws grant absolute protection to the therapist–client relationship, so in some circumstances a psychotherapist can be ordered by a judge to produce records or to testify involuntarily.

## Laws Limiting Confidentiality

### *Reporting Laws*

These state laws require the therapist to initiate a breach of confidentiality. The purpose of such laws is usually to protect someone else's safety or welfare. For example, abuse-reporting laws and duty-to-protect laws give a higher priority to another person's right to safety than to the client's right to confidentiality. These can include laws that protect rights such as the following:

- The right of a potential victim to be protected from harm by your client.
- The right of children or of elderly or incapacitated adults to be protected from abuse and neglect.
- The right of present and future clients to be protected from unprofessional or unethical conduct on the part of health care practitioners.

### *Laws Giving Others Access to Client Information Without Client Consent*

These laws do not require a therapist to initiate a disclosure or make a report, but they give others the legal right to obtain information without the client's consent. Most such laws arise at the state level and vary a great deal from state to state, making it important to learn those that apply in one's own state, but they can include laws such as the following:

- Parents may have the right to obtain information about a child client.
- A guardian ad litem in a court case may have access to information without consent.

- Evaluators for involuntary commitment hearings may have access to certain records.
- Social services investigators in child abuse cases may be legally free to obtain access to all relevant therapy records from any provider, whether or not that person made the report.
- State licensing boards conducting investigations of alleged professional misconduct may have subpoena power for obtaining treatment records relevant to their investigation.
- Third party payers may be legally free to redisclose certain information obtained from providers, sometimes to the agency or employer who has purchased the health care plan and (if the client later files an application for health or life insurance) to a national database.

At the federal level, the Patriot Act has sometimes been used to gain access to the treatment records of psychotherapy clients. In its earliest versions, psychotherapists were prohibited from notifying clients of such access, but more recent versions allow notifications of clients before the information is relinquished. (See American Psychological Association Practice Directorate, 2006; Munsey, 2006.)

### *Exceptions to Therapist–Client Privilege in Court Cases*

In every state, therapist–client privilege laws contain some exceptions that allow client information to be used as evidence in a court case. Most states make exceptions to privilege in child abuse cases and in cases where clients bring their own mental health into issue. A few states also have a "judicial discretion" exception to privilege—the broadest and least predictable exception to privilege—which allows any judge, in any case, to order a therapist to disclose client information.

The therapist–client privilege can also be abridged "secondhand" by statutes that allow others legal access to information obtained by therapists and then legally allow (or legally require) those others to testify about it. For example, evaluators for involuntary commitment or court-appointed special advocate volunteers in abuse cases may have legal access to records and then may later be legally allowed or required to testify about that information in the commitment hearing or child abuse court case.

### *Other Statutes Limiting Client Confidentiality in Specific Circumstances*

This category is defined broadly enough to include every state disclosure law that is not covered by the first three categories. This list would vary greatly from state to state. Some of the more obscure and "hidden" legal limitations of confidentiality fall into this category, but so do some of the familiar ones. You are responsible for knowing which of your own state's laws might fall into this category.

### Laws Allowing Disclosure

It is important not to confuse (a) laws that place actual legal limits on confidentiality (discussed earlier) with (b) laws that merely *allow* (but do not require) therapists to disclose information about their clients. Disclosures in the second category are *voluntary*—not legally required—meaning that therapists are legally free not to make those disclosures and clients are free not to give consent. This means they do not actually impose legal limits on confidentiality. For example, the HIPAA regulations *allow* broad types of disclosures without client authorization, but they *do not require* therapists to disclose anything. It is recommended here that psychotherapists make such disclosures only with the client's informed consent. (See the discussion of this distinction in the Introduction and in the Step 5 chapter, "Avoiding Preventable Disclosures"; see also Fisher, 2013.)

## FEDERAL HIPAA REGULATIONS AFFECTING CONFIDENTIALITY[2]

### HIPAA Rules

### *Privacy Rule*

This rule both imposes provider requirements and grants rights to health care clients.

[2]This section contains only excerpts from the federal HIPAA regulations. For links to complete text of HIPAA rules, see http://www.centerforethicalpractice.org/links-to-HIPAA-resources.

- Providers are required to take certain actions to protect privacy of client information.
- Providers must train their workforce about clients' confidentiality rights. (See the definition of *workforce*, discussed later.)
- Clients have certain rights about their own health care information, including (a) the right to receive "Notice of Privacy Practices" before consenting to services, (b) the right to review their own records, (c) the right to request amendments to their records, (d) the right to obtain copies of their records, (e) the right to request alternate forms of contact for communications, (f) the right to restrict certain disclosures of records or information, (g) the right to receive an accounting of all disclosures the provider has made, and (h) the right to complain of violations of these rights.

### *Security Rule*

Providers must follow certain guidelines for assuring security of confidential electronic client health information, including implementation of administrative, physical, and technical procedures. A policies and procedures document must be created and retained for 6 years. This must (a) document compliance with each step of implementation and (b) outline an emergency contingency plan (i.e., emergency mode operation plan, data backup plan, data recovery plan). These plans must be tested periodically.

### *Transaction Rule*

This rule standardizes the electronic exchange of identifiable client information for administrative and/or reimbursement purposes. Covered providers must obtain a National Provider Identifier for this purpose.

### *Enforcement Rule*

The privacy rule is enforced by the U.S. Office of Civil Rights. The security rule is enforced by the Center for Medicaid and Medicare Services. Civil penalties can be imposed for violations of these rules. A continuing violation may be deemed a separate violation for each day it occurs.

### *Breach Notification Rule*

Providers are required to report all their breaches of client information to the Department of Health and Human Services. Affected individuals must be notified by first-class mail; breaches involving 500 or more clients require media notices. See reporting requirements at http://www.gpo.gov/fdsys/pkg/FR-2013-01-25/pdf/2013-01073.pdf.

### *Omnibus ("Final") Rule*

This latest rule, enacted in 2013, amended the rules discussed previously and includes changes in privacy notice content and breach notification requirements (see http://www.centerforethicalpractice.org/links-to-HIPAA-resources).

Note that this rule requires that providers update their "Notice of Privacy Practices." The new version need not be given to existing clients who have already received a privacy notice. However, a copy of the updated privacy notice must be posted in the practitioner's office and all new clients must be given a copy. The HIPAA "Final Rule" stipulates that the updated "Notice of Privacy Practices" must include the following statements, among others:

- Uses and disclosures of patient information that are not described in the Privacy Notices will be made only with authorization from the individual.
- Patients have the right to restrict certain disclosures to health plans/insurance companies if the patient pays out of pocket in full for the health care service.
- Affected patients have the right to be notified following a breach of unsecured protected health information. (American Psychological Association Practice Organization, Legal and Regulatory Affairs Staff, 2013, para. 5)

### *HIPAA Requirement Regarding "Minimum Necessary" Disclosure of Confidential Client Information*

According to HIPAA (45 C.F.R. 164 514(d)),

> Minimum necessary uses of protected health information: (i) A covered entity must identify: (A) Those persons or classes of persons, as

appropriate, in its workforce who need access to protected health information to carry out their duties; and (B) For each such person or class of persons, the category or categories of protected health information to which access is needed and any conditions appropriate to such access. (ii) A covered entity must make reasonable efforts to limit the access of such persons or classes identified in paragraph (d)(2)(i)(A) of this section to protected health information consistent with paragraph (d)(2)(i)(B) of this section. . . . *Implementation specification*: Minimum necessary disclosures of protected health information: (i) For any type of disclosure that it makes on a routine and recurring basis, a covered entity must implement policies and procedures (which may be standard protocols) that limit the protected health information disclosed to the amount reasonably necessary to achieve the purpose of the disclosure. (ii) For all other disclosures, a covered entity must: (A) Develop criteria designed to limit the protected health information disclosed to the information reasonably necessary to accomplish the purpose for which disclosure is sought; and (B) Review requests for disclosure on an individual basis in accordance with such criteria.

### *HIPAA Staff Training Requirements*

Several of the HIPAA rules contain requirements about the training of staff:

- The *privacy rule* requires that personnel in health care settings receive training about confidentiality:

  *A covered entity must train all members of its workforce* [see the definition provided later] *on the policies and procedures with respect to protected health information . . . required by this subpart, as necessary and appropriate for the members of the workforce to carry out their function within the covered entity.* (45 CFR 184 530 (b) (1))

- The *security rule* also has implications for training. This rule requires the safeguarding of electronic client information to prevent unauthorized alteration, destruction, or disclosure of client information, whether intentional or unintentional. Providers must also create an emergency plan to address how employees should respond to a loss of electronic information in the event of a disaster or emergency.

- The *enforcement rule* describes circumstances under which a clinician may be held accountable for HIPAA violations by a workforce member or an "agent," unless the clinician required the workforce member or agent to sign a confidentiality contract explaining the HIPPA policies and the workforce member or agent broke it.

## HIPAA Definitions

- *Workforce*: Paid employees, trainees, supervisees, and volunteers who are under direct control of the HIPAA-covered clinician. It is not necessary for everyone to know *everything* about HIPAA and client privacy, but each should receive training necessary for carrying out his or her duties, including training about not accessing or handling client information beyond his or her job description and training, unless specifically so authorized. Therapists may use a written test or oral examination to ensure that the material is understood. We recommended that each member of the workforce be required to sign a confidentiality contract. If anyone who violates client confidentiality will be subject to disciplinary actions or will be removed from his or her position, this should be explicitly stated in the confidentiality contract.
- *Agent* or *business associate*: Anyone acting on the clinician's behalf and at his or her discretion, including billing services, accountants, answering services, and so forth. Contracted agents and business associates must sign a "business associates agreement" indicating that they understand and will abide by HIPAA-compliant privacy and confidentiality policies. You are usually not considered liable for their HIPAA violations if the business associates agreement clearly defines your expectations. However, you are not protected from liability for their violations if you knew that they failed to maintain the privacy or security obligations of that agreement and you failed to take reasonable steps to remedy the problem.

# Appendix D: Client Handout Template— "Limits of Confidentiality"

This template can serve both as an outline for a client handout describing the foreseeable limits of confidentiality and as a guide to discussing confidentiality's limits during the initial informed consent conversation.

## LIMITS IMPOSED VOLUNTARILY (i.e., NOT LEGALLY REQUIRED)

- Access to client information by others in the setting
  - Clinical colleagues in the setting (*include any with access to client information*)
  - Nonclinical employees in the setting (*include any with access to client information*)
  - Contracted agents (billing agents, answering service, computer guru, etc.)
- Other disclosures that the therapist may later make without further consent
  - Danger to self (*disclosure is voluntary in states where not legally required*)

The content of each section should contain details that are adapted to match the laws in your state and the policies in your setting.

  - Danger to others (*disclosure is voluntary in states where not legally required*)
  - Disclosure to parents about a minor client (*if voluntary in your state*)
  - Other
- Dual relationships or conflicts of interest that might compromise confidentiality
- Provider contracts that allow access by third party payers (*e.g., potential audits*)

## LIMITS IMPOSED BY LAW (i.e., POSSIBLE "INVOLUNTARY" DISCLOSURES)

- Laws requiring therapists to initiate disclosures without patient consent
  - Mandated reporting laws
  - Duty-to-warn or duty-to-protect laws
  - Other
- Laws granting others access to information without client consent (*varies by state*)
  - Parent access to minor child's treatment records (*if legally required*)
  - Access following mandated reports (*if legally allowed*)
  - Access in court cases involving child abuse (*e.g., court-appointed special advocate [CASA] laws*)
  - Access to information and records for involuntary commitment proceedings
  - Laws allowing recipients of information to rerelease without consent
  - Other
- Exceptions to therapist–client privilege (*examples only—exceptions vary by state*)
  - Client's mental health is at issue in the case
  - Cases involving child abuse
  - Custody or visitation disputes
  - "Judicial discretion"
  - Other

## POSSIBLE LIMITATIONS ON CONFIDENTIALITY CREATED BY USE OF TECHNOLOGY IN THE SETTING

- Situations when confidential information is stored on computers
- Circumstances when confidential information is transmitted electronically or faxed

## POSSIBLE REDISCLOSURE BY OTHERS OF INFORMATION A THERAPIST DISCLOSES TO THEM

- Client application for health or life insurance, mortgage or loan (*can trigger redisclosure of information previously disclosed to third party payers*)
- Redisclosures legally required (e.g., testimony by CASA worker, community service board evaluator)
- Redisclosures legally allowed (e.g., HIPAA-allowed sharing among providers)

# Appendix E: Elements of One-Way or Two-Way "Release of Information" Forms

***ONE-WAY RELEASE FORM.*** *Use this type of form if (a) you want to obtain client's consent to* ***release information*** *to someone who will not be releasing information to you or (b) you want to* ***obtain information*** *about the client from another person without disclosing any information beyond identifying the client (e.g., obtaining consent for a previous therapist to give you information).*

Identifying information:

Name of person whose information will be released ____________________
DOB_____

The person named above has given consent for me to [check one]

___ provide confidential information to the following person **or**

___ obtain information from the following person

Name ________________________________________________

Contact information (e.g., address, phone) ____________________

Specific information to be disclosed ______________________________

Purpose for the disclosure (e.g., diagnosis, treatment planning, coordination of services) ________________________________________________

________________________________________________________________

Expiration date (the date beyond which this consent will expire and must be renewed) ______________________________________________

Signature of patient or client (or person authorized to give consent, if different)

***TWO-WAY RELEASE FORM.*** *Use this type of form if you want to exchange information about the client with another person (e.g., when obtaining a client's consent to have an ongoing two-way exchange of information with a current physician or referring agency).*

Identifying information:

Name of person whose information will be released ___________________
DOB______

The person named above has given consent for information to be exchanged between me and:

Name ______________________________________________________

Contact information (e.g., address, phone) ___________________

Specific information to be disclosed in that exchange___________________

Purpose for the disclosure (e.g., diagnosis, treatment planning, coordination of services) ______________________________________________________

______________________________________________________

Expiration date (the date beyond which this consent will expire and must be renewed) ______________________________________________________

Signature of patient or client (or person authorized to give consent, if different)

# Appendix F: Ethical Responsibilities in Legal Contexts

## PREPARING TO RESPOND ETHICALLY TO LEGAL DEMANDS FOR CLIENT INFORMATION

Learn and prepare to cite the laws that are protective of client confidentiality.

- How will this law help you protect confidential information?
- When is it helpful to cite your state's nondisclosure statutes and regulations?
- When is it helpful to cite your state's therapist–client privilege laws?
- In federal court cases, do you remember to invoke *Jaffee v. Redmond?*

Learn and understand the implications of each law unprotective of confidentiality.

- What does this law ask you to do regarding clients' confidential information?
- What is the potential impact of this law on a therapy client?
- What ethical concerns does this law therefore raise for therapists?
- What legal options are available for responding in the most ethical manner?
- What are the legal or financial penalties (if any) for "ignoring" this law?
- How will you explain this law to prospective patients or clients (see Step 2)?

Create a plan for responding ethically to the unprotective laws and regulations.

- Laws requiring you to make reports or otherwise initiate disclosures
  Be clear about what each law actually requires
  - Reporting laws
  - Duty-to-protect laws
  - Other laws that can limit confidentiality

  Understand the legal options for responding to each law
  - How can you limit the amount of information you disclose?
  - If it requires a report, can it be made anonymously?
  - If a report is required, can the client report to protect the relationship?
- Laws granting others access to client information without client consent
  Differentiate between legally required and legally allowed ("voluntary").
  Inform client both in advance and when the circumstance arises (Step 2).
- Laws allowing recipients of information to redisclose without client consent
  Inform client about this possibility in advance (Step 2).
  Discuss this when obtaining consent for any voluntary disclosure (Step 3).
- Exceptions to therapist–client privilege in court cases
  Inform client about this possibility in advance (Step 2).
  *Know the difference between a subpoena and a court order* (discussed later).
  Advise the client (or ex-client) as soon as you receive a subpoena.
  Determine whether the client wishes the information to be used as evidence in case.
  If so, obtain written consent before providing the information.
  If not, with consent, collaborate with the client's attorney to protect.

(Also see resources and citations in Step 1 and Step 4 chapters.)

# DISTINGUISHING BETWEEN SUBPOENAS AND COURT ORDERS[1]

Ethically, the legal difference between a subpoena and a court order becomes critically important.

> A subpoena *simply compels a response* [emphasis added], and in some jurisdictions an attorney can obtain one simply by asking the court clerk. . . . A court order, on the other hand, typically flows from a hearing before a judge and *compels a disclosure* [emphasis added] unless appealed in a higher court. In the end, the court must decide what qualifies as protected or not. (Koocher & Keith-Spiegel, 2008, pp. 209–210)

## Subpoenas

In preparing for a court case, attorneys may issue "discovery" subpoenas in an attempt to uncover potential evidence prior to a formal court proceeding. This could be in the form of a *subpoena duces tecum* (for client records or other physical evidence) or a witness subpoena (to request that the therapist give a deposition). Later, a psychotherapist may receive a witness subpoena demanding courtroom testimony. Although a psychotherapist is legally required to take some action in response to receiving a subpoena, it is ethically important to remember that subpoenas can be issued without a judge's knowledge, do not carry the legal weight of a court order, and can be overturned by a judge (Fisher, 2013).

## Court Orders

A court order may look similar to a subpoena, but legally it is a different document, and this has important ethical implications (Fisher, 2013). A

[1] For a more detailed discussion of the issues in this section, see Fisher (2013). For examples of state-specific recommendations, see Florida (Florida Psychological Association, n.d.), Pennsylvania (Baturin, Knapp, & Tepper, 2003), and Virginia (Fisher, 2007).

court order will indicate on the document (usually on the first page) that it is an "order of the court," and it will be signed by the judge whose name is included on the order, not by an attorney or a court clerk. In other words, this request for evidence has been reviewed by a judge who can either order that the requested information be disclosed or can issue a protective order that prevents it from being used as evidence. "If you are not sure whether the document is a court order, you may contact the court that issued the document and ask to speak to the judge's clerk" (American Psychological Association [APA] Practice Organization, Legal and Regulatory Affairs Staff, 2008, p. 3).

## AVOIDING UNWANTED SUBPOENAS

It can be impossible to avoid all involuntary involvement with the legal system, especially in states with weak therapist–client privilege laws, but the following are some ways to lessen the likelihood of receiving an unwanted subpoena in the first place:

- Psychotherapists are free to screen prospective cases carefully and refuse to begin relationships with individuals, couples, or families who are involved in court proceedings (or likely headed for court), on the basis that they do not have forensic training or experience in court procedures and are not interested in the "hybrid" role of therapist and assistant to the court.
- Gottlieb and Coleman (2012) suggested the use of intake forms stipulating that "the clinician does not offer expert testimony" (p. 119). Prospective clients who hope to have a therapist who will provide depositions or testimony can be referred to therapists who have forensic training or experience with court procedures.
- Fisher (2004) provided "nonsubpoena forms" to be signed by prospective clients, in which clients agree that the therapy services are to be provided only for clinical purposes and promise not to subpoena the psychologist or the records for legal purposes. Although these signatures are not legally binding and might not be enforced by a court (APA Committee on Legal Issues, 2006; Bennett et al., 2006), they can nevertheless

reduce the likelihood that clients will naively encourage or allow their attorney to subpoena their therapist. There is anecdotal evidence that judges sometimes take this promise into consideration when deciding whether to order testimony from a therapist who is subpoenaed by one member of a couple in a divorce case or by one of the parents in a custody case.

## RESPONDING ETHICALLY TO SUBPOENAS

The first step in the ethical practice model involves "preparation." The Step 1 chapter in this manual contains a checklist that includes some of the advance preparations that might be required based on the legal options available in your state for responding to subpoenas in various circumstances.

To protect confidentiality to the extent legally possible, as advocated in this manual, therapists must contest a subpoena if the client does not want the information disclosed. "In most states, you can turn over the documents or show up to testify without obtaining your client's consent *only* if the subpoena you received qualifies as a court order from a judge, which is rare" (APA Practice Organization, Legal and Regulatory Affairs Staff, 2008, p. 3). In other words, in the context of legal proceedings, your ethical rule of thumb can be not to voluntarily turn over information in the absence of client consent without a court order. Not only is this important as ethical advice but The Trust, a malpractice insurer, has suggested that it is also good risk-management advice: "In general, a psychologist may only disclose information with the consent of the patient or in response to a court order. *The receipt of a subpoena alone without the consent of the patient does not override this requirement* [emphasis added]" (Bennett et al., 2006, p. 111). Depending on your state's laws, this can also be important legal advice. For example, one state court imposed a fine of $100,000 when patient information was disclosed without the patient's consent in the context of a court case, but in the absence of a court's order (see *Fairfax Hospital v. Patricia Curtis*, 1997).

For therapists who are unfamiliar with subpoenas and unsure about the possible responses, the first thing to do in response to a subpoena is *nothing*. Note that you must not maintain this posture for too long because subpoenas offer limited response times. But if you are not adequately prepared and do not understand your legal options, pause long enough to obtain consultation before acting to ensure that your first move is not one that limits the client's confidentiality rights unnecessarily. Although state laws vary, the following would usually be among the first recommended actions:[2] (a) Clarify who sent the subpoena and what it is demanding and (b) notify the client that the subpoena has been received.

- In interacting with the client, the legal staff of the APA Practice Organization advised as follows:

  > If the document is not a court order (the first subpoena you receive in a matter rarely is a court order), you will need to obtain your client's consent or authorization before turning over confidential information. This step is required because most state and federal jurisdictions recognize a psychotherapist–patient privilege that allows the client to prevent confidential material from being disclosed to others. . . . When obtaining this consent, you should tell your client exactly what you have been asked to turn over and explain that there is no guarantee that the information will be kept confidential. . . . The written consent that you obtain from your client should contain, at a minimum: Exactly what information will be disclosed; to whom the information will be disclosed (for example, to the requesting attorney); the purpose of the disclosure (to respond to a subpoena); the client's signature and date. (APA Practice Organization, Legal and Regulatory Affairs Staff, 2008, p. 3)

- If the client does not wish the information to be disclosed, obtain consent from the client to consult with the client's attorney about a planned response. If the client has no attorney, you can advise the client that the subpoena can be legally contested and/or you can proceed to contest

[2] For a more detailed discussion of each of these options, see Chapter 7, "Responding Ethically to Legal Demands for 'Involuntary' Disclosure of Patient Information," in Fisher (2013).

the subpoena on the client's behalf (if state law so allows). "If a psychotherapist believes that a request for records violates confidentiality, he or she should assert the privilege on behalf of the client and let the respective court resolve it" (Younggren & Harris, 2008, p. 599).

- In the absence of the client's explicit consent to disclose the requested information, the most ethical position is to refuse to disclose anything unless a judge orders you to disclose it. To obtain a judge's decision, someone must file a motion with the court (usually a "motion to quash" a subpoena or a "motion to limit disclosure"). Following a hearing, the judge may issue (a) a protective order or (b) an order that the subpoenaed documents (or testimony) be provided. In the face of a court order to disclose the information, a psychotherapist will have few legal options other than compliance. Noncompliance can lead to fines and/or incarceration for contempt of court.

> In contrast to a subpoena, a court order, issued by a judge following a review of the request at hand, *does* [emphasis added] override the need to obtain patient consent. . . . In most instances, compliance with a court order is indicated. In the rare situation where the psychologist may wish to challenge the issuance of the court order, legal counsel will be necessary to avoid an indirect or direct appearance of contemptuous behavior. (Baturin, Knapp, & Tepper, 2003, pp. 1–2)

- A psychotherapist who is court ordered to provide testimony "involuntarily" may have one further decision to make—whether to testify as a "fact witness" or an "expert witness." The former is usually more protective of client confidentiality (see Fisher, 2013, Chapter 12).

## CLARIFYING YOUR COURT-RELATED ROLES AND THEIR ETHICAL IMPLICATIONS

In Table F.1, the final column indicates some of the differential ethical obligations that accompany certain voluntary and involuntary roles undertaken by psychotherapists in court cases.

**Table F.1**

**Which Hat Are You Wearing? Differential Ethical Obligations in Voluntary and Involuntary Court-Related Roles**

| Voluntary roles | Possible activities | Informed consent obligations and other ethical duties |
|---|---|---|
| 1. Therapist (participating at client's request and/ or with client's written consent) | A. Providing records or other documents<br>B. Providing deposition or courtroom testimony<br>Fact witness<br>"Expert" (opinion) witness<br>C. Consulting with patient's attorney | 1. Before obtaining client's consent to disclose records or provide testimony, inform client about the content of the records and/or about the information that may be disclosed in deposition or testimony, explain that a cross-examination may cover any aspect of therapy, note possible types of questions that can be asked and indicate how you might answer, explain that you must answer questions truthfully and that you may not provide only positive information as if you were simply a "good character witness."<br>2. Obtain client's informed consent before disclosing anything to client's attorney. (Client's attorney may say this is legally unnecessary, but ethically, there is no basis for disclosing anything to anyone without client's written consent unless court so orders.) |
| 2. Provider of court-ordered intervention services (clinician agrees to wear this "hat," but client is participating "involuntarily") | A. Providing court-ordered services (e.g., therapy, co-parenting consultation, parent education, mediation)<br>B. Providing records, reports, or testimony about the services provided | 1. Note that in this "hybrid" role, you wear two hats, because you have responsibilities to both the client and to the court. Judges can order people to obtain services, but you are not legally required to be the one who provides those services. If you decline, give court your reasons. You are ethically required to refuse if (a) it creates an unethical dual relationship or (b) you are not trained to provide the service or are unfamiliar with court roles and procedures, and so forth.<br>2. In advance, clarify court's expectations to ensure that they match the services and disclosure conditions you are willing to agree to. Before providing services, inform prospective client of the scope of the court's order and explain the limits of confidentiality it imposes, including expected or foreseeable disclosures to the court. |

| Involuntary role | Possible activities | Informed consent obligations and other ethical duties |
|---|---|---|
| 3. Therapist or former therapist (subpoenaed by opposing party or by client's own attorney; court has ordered you to participate against client's wishes and without client consent) | (If judge refuses to quash the subpoena and instead orders you to participate)<br>A. Providing records or other documents (subpoena duces tecum)<br>B. Providing deposition or courtroom testimony (witness subpoena)<br>1. Fact witness (testimony limited to client's statements, behavior, etc.)<br>2. Opinion ("expert") witness (e.g., testimony regarding opinion, diagnosis, prognosis) | 1. At intake, inform all prospective clients about the potential limits of confidentiality, including those imposed by exceptions in your state's therapist–client privilege laws. In most states, these will include (a) child abuse or neglect cases or (b) cases in which client places own mental condition at issue, but exceptions vary state to state, and some states have much broader exceptions.<br>Note that it is unclear on whose behalf you are wearing this hat. Obviously, you are not participating in behalf of your client, whose confidential information you are about to disclose against his or her wishes and without his or her consent. But remember that, unlike a forensic specialist who participates voluntarily, you are not here to act on behalf of the court. Your relationship with this client began for clinical reasons unrelated to court proceedings, and you are not here wearing a neutral hat. You will enter the court proceedings wearing a therapist hat, and your loyalty remains with the client.<br>2. Your primary responsibility is to your client, who did not consent for you to wear this hat.<br>3. Remember, a subpoena is not a court order. It is not ethically appropriate to disclose information in response to a subpoena alone, so first file (or with client consent, join client's attorney in filing) a motion to quash the subpoena. If judge orders you to disclose, limit the disclosure to the extent legally possible.<br>4. Give no testimony or opinion about anyone other than the client named in the court order unless (a) you saw him or her in therapy or evaluated him or her and (b) he or she has given consent to this disclosure. |

*Note.* This chart does not include the hybrid "treating expert" roles in which psychotherapists provide clinical services to a court-involved couple or family and begin the clinical relationship by explaining that they will also be assisting the court in its decision making in their court case. Adapted from "Which Hat Are You Wearing? Roles & Ethical Responsibilities of Mental Health Professionals in Court Cases," by the Center for Ethical Practice, 2014, available online at http://www.centerforethicalpractice.org/Which-Hat. Copyright 2014 by Mary Alice Fisher. See also the more extensive chart in Appendix VI of Fisher (2013).

# Appendix G: Protecting Clients' Confidentiality Rights—An Annotated Version of the Ethical Practice Model

Showing How State Laws and Regulations and Federal HIPAA Regulations Fit Into This Ethical Model[1]

## STEP 1. PREPARE

1. Understand Clients' Rights and Your Ethical Responsibilities on Behalf of Those Rights.
2. *Learn Laws Affecting Confidentiality (Refer to Step 4).*
   *State Laws, Regulations, and Court Cases*
   *Federal Laws and Regulations and Court Cases (e.g., HIPAA)*
3. Clarify Your Own Personal Ethical Position About Confidentiality and Its Limits.
   Decide when you will disclose client information "voluntarily."
   *Plan your response to each law that can require you to disclose "involuntarily."*
4. Find Reliable Ethics Consultants and Legal Consultants and Use Them as Needed.

[1] Italics indicate how laws and legal requirements fit into the model. Adapted from "Confidentiality: Using An Ethical Practice Model to Integrate Ethical Standards, State Laws, & HIPAA," by the Center for Ethical Practice, 2010, available online at http://www.centerforethicalpractice.org/EthicalPracticeModelAnnotated. Copyright 2010 by Mary Alice Fisher.

5. Devise Informed Consent Forms That Reflect Your *Actual* Policies and Intentions.
   *HIPAA "Notice of Privacy Practices"*
   Personalized bulleted list of "limits of confidentiality" in your setting
6. Prepare to Discuss Confidentiality and Its Limits With Clients in Understandable Language.

## STEP 2. TELL PROSPECTIVE CLIENTS THE TRUTH (INFORM THEIR CONSENT)

1. Inform Prospective Clients About Limits of Confidentiality That Apply to All Clients.
   Limits imposed voluntarily
   *Limits imposed by laws*
2. Explain Any Roles or Potential Conflicts of Interest That Might Affect Confidentiality.
3. Obtain Informed Client's Consent About These Potential Limits of Confidentiality.
   Inform prospective client of potential "conditions" on confidentiality.
   Obtain client's consent to accept these as a condition of receiving services.
   Document this informed consent process.
4. Reopen the Conversation if Client's Circumstances, Laws, or Your Intentions Change.

## STEP 3. OBTAIN "TRULY INFORMED CONSENT" BEFORE DISCLOSING VOLUNTARILY

1. Disclose Information Without Client Consent Only if *Legally Unavoidable.*
2. Inform Client Adequately About the Nature and Implications of the Proposed Disclosure.
3. Obtain and Document the Client's Signed Consent Before Disclosing the Information.

## STEP 4. RESPOND ETHICALLY TO LEGAL DEMANDS FOR INFORMATION

1. *Notify Client of Pending Legal Requirement to Disclose Information Without Client Consent.*
2. *Respond Ethically to Legal Obligations (According to Plan Devised in Step 1).*
3. *Limit Disclosure to the Extent Legally Possible.*

## STEP 5. AVOID PREVENTABLE BREACHES OF CONFIDENTIALITY

1. Establish and Maintain Protective Policies and Procedures in the Office, Institution, or Agency.
2. Avoid "Informal" Discussions, "Unofficial" Disclosures, and Casual Conversations About Clients.
3. Monitor Record-Keeping Practices, *Conduct HIPAA-Compliant Staff Training.*
4. Avoid Dual Roles That Create Conflicts of Interest in the Courtroom and Elsewhere.
5. *Anticipate Legal Demands, Empower Clients to Act Protectively on Their Own Behalf.*
6. *Do Not Confuse Laws That Permit Me to Disclose With Laws That Legally Require Disclosure.*

## STEP 6. TALK ABOUT CONFIDENTIALITY: EDUCATE EACH OTHER AND OTHERS

1. Go Public: Refuse to Keep Confidentiality Problems a Secret.
2. Model Ethical Practices: Confront Others' Unethical Practices.
3. Teach Ethical Practices to Employees, Students, Supervisees, and Agency Administrators.
4. Educate Attorneys, Judges, and the Public About the Importance of Confidentiality in Therapy.

5. *Explore Possibilities for Legislative Change Toward More Protective Confidentiality Laws.*
6. Develop Multidisciplinary Training, Continuing Education, and Consultation.

# References

Acuff, C., Bennett, B. E., Bricklin, P. M., Canter, M. B., Knapp, S. J., Moldawsky, S., & Phelps, R. (1999). Considerations for ethical practice in managed care. *Professional Psychology: Research and Practice, 30*, 563–575. http://dx.doi.org/10.1037/0735-7028.30.6.563

American Association for Marriage and Family Therapy. (2001). *Code of ethics.* Alexandria, VA: Author. Retrieved from http://www.aamft.org/imis15/Content/Legal_Ethics/Code_of_Ethics.aspx

American Counseling Association. (2014). *ACA code of ethics.* Retrieved from http://www.counseling.org/docs/ethics/2014-aca-code-of-ethics.pdf?sfvrsn=4

American Psychiatric Association. (2009). *The principles of medical ethics with annotations especially applicable to psychiatry.* Retrieved from http://www.psychiatry.org/practice/ethics

American Psychological Association. (2010). *Ethical principles of psychologists and code of conduct (2002, Amended June 1, 2010).* Retrieved from http://www.apa.org/ethics/code/index.aspx

American Psychological Association. (2013). Specialty guidelines for forensic psychology. *American Psychologist, 68*, 7–19. http://dx.doi.org/10.1037/a0029889

American Psychological Association Committee on Legal Issues. (2006). Strategies for private practitioners coping with subpoenas or compelled testimony for client records or test data. *Professional Psychology: Research and Practice, 27*, 215–222. http://content.apa.org/journals/pro/37/2/215.pdf

American Psychological Association Practice Directorate. (2006). *Patriot Act renewal tightens medical records safeguards.* Retrieved from https://apa.org/about/division/officers/dialogue/2006/05/practice.aspx

American Psychological Association Practice Organization, Legal and Regulatory Affairs Staff. (2005a). *Managed care record audits.* Retrieved from http://www.apapracticecentral.org/business/legal/professional/secure/record-audits.aspx

American Psychological Association Practice Organization, Legal and Regulatory Affairs Staff. (2005b). *Managing your managed care contracts.* Retrieved from http://www.apapracticecentral.org/business/legal/professional/secure/managed-care-contract.aspx

American Psychological Association Practice Organization, Legal and Regulatory Affairs Staff. (2008). *How to deal with a subpoena.* Retrieved from http://www.apapracticecentral.org/update/2008/12-17/subpoena.aspx

American Psychological Association Practice Organization, Legal and Regulatory Affairs Staff. (2013). *HIPAA Final Rule highlights for practitioners.* Retrieved from http://www.apapracticecentral.org/update/2013/03-14/final-rule.aspx

Appelbaum, P. S., Lidz, C. W., & Meisel, A. (1987). *Informed consent: Legal theory and clinical practice.* New York, NY: Oxford University Press.

Bailey, D. S. (2003, October). Ethics as prevention. *Monitor on Psychology*, *34*, 68.

Barnett, J. E. (2012, March). Clinical writing about clients: Is informed consent sufficient? *Psychotherapy*, *49*, 12–15. http://dx.doi.org/10.1037/a0025249

Barnett, J. E., Wise, E. H., Johnson-Greene, D., & Bucky, S. F. (2007). Informed consent: Too much of a good thing or not enough? *Professional Psychology: Research and Practice*, *38*, 179–186. http://dx.doi.org/10.1037/0735-7028.38.2.179

Barnett, J. E., Zimmerman, J. Z., & Walfish, S. (2014). *Ethics in private practice: A practical guide for mental health clinicians.* New York, NY: Oxford University Press.

Baturin, R. L., Knapp, S. J., & Tepper, A. M. (2003). Practical considerations when responding to subpoenas and court orders. *Pennsylvania Psychologist*, *63*(8), 1–2.

Beahrs, J. O., & Gutheil, T. G. (2001). Informed consent in psychotherapy. *The American Journal of Psychiatry*, *158*, 4–10. http://dx.doi.org/10.1176/appi.ajp.158.1.4

Beck, J. C. (1990). The basic issues. In J. C. Beck (Ed.), *Confidentiality versus the duty to protect: Foreseeable harm in the practice of psychiatry* (pp. 1–8). Washington, DC: American Psychiatric Press.

Beeman, D. G., & Scott, N. A. (1991). Therapists' attitudes toward psychotherapy informed consent with adolescents. *Professional Psychology: Research and Practice*, *22*, 230–234. http://dx.doi.org/10.1037/0735-7028.22.3.230

Behnke, S. (2004, September). Disclosures of confidential information under the new APA Ethics Code: A process for deciding when and how. *Monitor on Psychology*, *35*, 78–79.

Bennett, B. E., Bricklin, P. M., Harris, E., Knapp, S., VandeCreek, L., & Younggren, J. N. (2006). *Assessing and managing risk in psychological practice: An individualized approach.* Rockville, MD: American Psychological Association Insurance Trust. http://dx.doi.org/10.1037/14293-000

Beyer, K. (2000, September). First person: *Jaffe v. Redmond* therapist speaks. *American Psychoanalyst, 34.* Retrieved from http://jaffee-redmond.org/articles/beyer.htm

Bollas, C., & Langs, R. (1999). It is time to take a stand. *Newsletter of the International Psychoanalytical Association, 8,* pp. 1, 7–8.

Bollas, C., & Sundelson, D. (1995). *The new informants: The betrayal of confidentiality in psychoanalysis and psychotherapy.* Northvale, NJ: Jason Aronson.

Center for Ethical Practice. (2006). *Ethical obligations about informed consent.* Retrieved from http://www.centerforethicalpractice.org/ethical-obligations-informed-consent/

Center for Ethical Practice. (2009). *Staff training: Sample documents.* Retrieved from http://www.centerforethicalpractice.org/staff-training

Center for Ethical Practice. (2010). *Confidentiality: Using an ethical practice model to integrate ethical standards, state laws, & HIPAA.* Retrieved from http://www.centerforethicalpractice.org/EthicalPracticeModelAnnotated

Center for Ethical Practice. (2012). *Record keeping—Resources from national professional associations.* Retrieved from http://www.centerforethicalpractice.org/record-keeping-resources/

Center for Ethical Practice. (2013). *Examples of federal and state laws affecting confidentiality.* Retrieved from http://www.centerforethicalpractice.org/lawsaffectingconfidentiality

Center for Ethical Practice. (2014a). *Ethical practice model adapted to various settings & tasks.* Retrieved from http://www.centerforethicalpractice.org/EthicalPracticeModel_Adapted

Center for Ethical Practice. (2014b). *Which hat are you wearing? Roles & ethical responsibilities of mental health professionals in court cases.* Retrieved from http://www.centerforethicalpractice.org/Which-Hat

Childress-Beatty, L., & Koocher, G. P. (2013). Dealing with subpoenas. In G. P. Koocher, J. C. Norcross, & B. A. Greene (Eds.), *Psychologists' desk reference* (3rd ed., pp. 564–567). New York, NY: Oxford University Press. http://dx.doi.org/10.1093/med:psych/9780199845491.003.0107

Cooper, C. C., & Gottlieb, M. C. (2000). Ethical issues with managed care: Challenges facing counseling psychology. *The Counseling Psychologist, 28,* 179–236. http://tcp.sagepub.com/cgi/content/abstract/28/2/179. http://dx.doi.org/10.1177/0011000000282001

Davidson, J. R., & Davidson, T. (1996). Confidentiality and managed care: Ethical and legal concerns. *Health & Social Work, 21*, 208–215.

Donner, M. B., VandeCreek, L., Gonsiorek, J. C., & Fisher, C. B. (2008). Balancing confidentiality: Protecting privacy and protecting the public. *Professional Psychology: Research and Practice, 39*, 369–376. http://dx.doi.org/10.1037/0735-7028.39.3.369

Epstein, R. S. (1994). *Keeping boundaries: Maintaining safety and integrity in the psychotherapeutic process.* Washington, DC: American Psychiatric Press.

Fairfax Hospital v. Patricia Curtis, 254 Va. 437 (1997).

Federal Evidence Review. (2015). *Federal Rules of Evidence 2015.* Retrieved from http://federalevidence.com/downloads/rules.of.evidence.pdf

Fisher, M. A. (2004). *Sample non-subpoena contract.* Retrieved from http://www.centerforethicalpractice.org/sample-non-subpoena-contract/

Fisher, M. A. (2005). *Ethical decision-making model.* Retrieved from http://www.centerforethicalpractice.org/ethical-decision-making-model/

Fisher, M. A. (2006). *Confidentiality ethics: Yesterday and today.* Retrieved from http://www.centerforethicalpractice.org/conditionalconfidentialityethics

Fisher, M. A. (2007). *Ethical and legal responsibilities of Virginia mental health professionals in response to a subpoena.* Retrieved from http://www.centerforethicalpractice.org/Virginia-RespondingToSubpoenas

Fisher, M. A. (2008). Protecting confidentiality rights: The need for an ethical practice model. *American Psychologist, 63*, 1–13. http://dx.doi.org/10.1037/0003-066X.63.1.1

Fisher, M. A. (2009a). Ethics-based training for non-clinical staff in mental health settings. *Professional Psychology: Research and Practice, 40*, 459–466. http://dx.doi.org/10.1037/a0016642

Fisher, M. A. (2009b). Replacing "Who is the client?" with a different ethical question. *Professional Psychology: Research and Practice, 40*, 1–7. http://dx.doi.org/10.1037/a0014011

Fisher, M. A. (2012). Confidentiality and record keeping. In S. J. Knapp, M. C. Gottlieb, M. M. Handelsman, & L. D. VandeCreek (Eds.), *APA handbook of ethics in psychology* (Vol. 1, pp. 333–375). Washington, DC: American Psychological Association. http://dx.doi.org/10.1037/13271-013

Fisher, M. A. (2013). *The ethics of conditional confidentiality: A practice model for mental health professionals.* New York, NY: Oxford University Press. http://dx.doi.org/10.1093/med/9780199752201.001.0001

Fisher, M. A. (2014). Why "Who is the client?" is the wrong ethical question. *Journal of Applied School Psychology, 30*, 183–208. http://dx.doi.org/10.1080/15377903.2014.888531

Fisher, M. A., & the Center for Ethical Practice. (2008). Protecting confidentiality rights: The need for an ethical practice model. *American Psychologist*, *63*, 1–13. http://www.centerforethicalpractice.org/publications/articles-mary-alice-fisher/protecting-confidentiality-rights

Florida Psychological Association. (n.d.). *Subpoenas and court orders for documents and oral deposition in Florida civil cases.* Retrieved from https://flapsych.site-ym.com/store/ViewProduct.aspx?id=2117334&hhSearchTerms=%2522subpoena%2522

Forester-Miller, H., & Davis, T. (1996). *A practitioner's guide to ethical decision making.* Retrieved from http://www.counseling.org/docs/ethics/practitioners_guide.pdf?sfvrsn=2

Gottlieb, M. C., & Coleman, A. (2012). Ethical challenges in forensic psychology practice. In S. J. Knapp, M. C. Gottlieb, M. M. Handelsman, & L. D. VandeCreek (Eds.), *APA handbook of ethics in psychology* (Vol. 2, pp. 91–123). Washington, DC: American Psychological Association. http://dx.doi.org/10.1037/13272-006

Haas, L. J., & Malouf, J. L. (2005). *Keeping up the good work: A practitioner's guide to mental health ethics* (4th ed.). Sarasota, FL: Professional Resource Press.

Haggerty, L. A., & Hawkins, J. (2000). Informed consent and the limits of confidentiality. *Western Journal of Nursing Research*, *22*, 508–514. http://dx.doi.org/10.1177/01939450022044557

Handelsman, M. M., Kemper, M. B., Kesson-Craig, P., McLain, J., & Johnsrud, C. (1986). Use, content, and readability of written informed consent forms for treatment. *Professional Psychology: Research and Practice*, *17*, 514–518. http://dx.doi.org/10.1037/0735-7028.17.6.514

Handelsman, M. M., & Martin, W. L., Jr. (1992). Effects of readability on the impact and recall of written informed consent material. *Professional Psychology: Research and Practice*, *23*, 500–503. http://dx.doi.org/10.1037/0735-7028.23.6.500

Harris, E., & Bennett, B. E. (1999). *Sample informed consent form.* Retrieved from http://www.trustinsurance.com/resources/download-documents

Harris, E., & Younggren, J. (2011, July–August). But that's what the lawyer told me. *The National Psychologist*, pp. 13, 17.

HIPAA. (2013, January 25). "Final Rule" (Modification of 45 CFR Parts 160 and 164). *Federal Register*, *78*(17). Retrieved from http://www.gpo.gov/fdsys/pkg/FR-2013-01-25/pdf/2013-01073.pdf

Hochhauser, M. (1999). Informed consent and patient's rights documents: A right, a rite, or a rewrite? *Ethics & Behavior*, *9*, 1–20. http://dx.doi.org/10.1207/s15327019eb0901_1

Jaffee v. Redmond, 116 S. Ct. 95–266, 641, W. 4490 (1996).

Joseph, D., & Onek, J. (1999). Confidentiality in psychiatry. In S. Bloch, P. Chodoff, & S. A. Green (Eds.), *Psychiatric ethics* (3rd ed., pp. 105–140). New York, NY: Oxford University Press.

Kipnis, K. (2003, October). In defense of absolute confidentiality. *The Virtual Mentor*, *5*(10). Retrieved from http://virtualmentor.ama-assn.org/2003/10/hlaw2-0310.html

Knapp, S. (2002, April). Accidental breaches of confidentiality. *Pennsylvania Psychologist*, *62*, 6–7.

Knapp, S., Gottlieb, M., Berman, J., & Handelsman, M. M. (2007). When laws and ethics collide: What should psychologists do? *Professional Psychology: Research and Practice*, *38*, 54–59. http://dx.doi.org/10.1037/0735-7028.38.1.54

Knapp, S. J., & VandeCreek, L. D. (2012). *Practical ethics for psychologists: A positive approach* (2nd ed.). Washington, DC: American Psychological Association.

Koman, S. L., & Harris, E. A. (2005). Contracting with managed care organizations. In G. P. Koocher, J. C. Norcross, & S. S. Hill III (Eds.), *Psychologists' desk reference* (2nd ed., pp. 653–657). New York, NY: Oxford University Press.

Koocher, G. P., & Keith-Spiegel, P. (2008). *Ethics in psychology and the mental health professions: Standards and cases* (3rd ed.). New York, NY: Oxford University Press.

Koocher, G. P., & Keith-Spiegel, P. (2009). *What should I do?—39 ethical dilemmas involving confidentiality.* Retrieved from http://www.continuingedcourses.net/active/courses/course049.php

Kraft, S. (2005). *Adolescent informed consent form.* Retrieved from http://www.centerforethicalpractice.org/Form-AdolescentConsent

Kuo, F.-C. (2009). Secrets or no secrets: Confidentiality in couple therapy. *American Journal of Family Therapy*, *37*, 351–354. http://dx.doi.org/10.1080/01926180701862970

Langs, R. (1998). *Ground rules in psychotherapy and counseling.* London, England: Karnac Books.

Langs, R. (2008). Unconscious death anxiety and the two modes of psychotherapy. *Psychoanalytic Review*, *95*, 791–818. http://dx.doi.org/10.1521/prev.2008.95.5.791

Lasky, G. B., & Riva, M. T. (2006). Confidentiality and privileged communication in group psychotherapy. *International Journal of Group Psychotherapy*, *56*, 455–476. http://dx.doi.org/10.1521/ijgp.2006.56.4.455

Mattison, M. (2000). Ethical decision making: The person in the process. *Social Work*, *45*, 201–212. http://dx.doi.org/10.1093/sw/45.3.201

Munsey, C. (2006, April). More protection for psychologists' records in renewed Patriot Act. *Monitor on Psychology*, *37*(4), 15.

National Association of Social Workers. (2008). *Code of ethics.* Washington, DC: Author.

Nowell, D., & Spruill, J. (1993). If it's not absolutely confidential, will information be disclosed? *Professional Psychology: Research and Practice, 24,* 367–369. http://dx.doi.org/10.1037/0735-7028.24.3.367

Paradise, L. V., & Kirby, P. C. (1990). Some perspectives on the legal liability of group counseling in private practice. *Journal for Specialists in Group Work, 15,* 114–118. http://dx.doi.org/10.1080/01933929008411920

Pomerantz, A. M., & Handelsman, M. M. (2004). Informed consent revisited: An updated written question format. *Professional Psychology, Research and Practice, 35,* 201–205. http://dx.doi.org/10.1037/0735-7028.35.2.201

Pope, K. S., & Bajt, T. R. (1988). When laws and values conflict: A dilemma for psychologists. *American Psychologist, 43,* 828–829. http://dx.doi.org/10.1037/0003-066X.43.10.828

Pope, K. S., & Vasquez, M. J. T. (2005). *How to survive and thrive as a therapist: Information, ideas, and resources for psychologists in practice.* Washington, DC: American Psychological Association. http://dx.doi.org/10.1037/11088-000

Pope, K. S., & Vasquez, M. J. T. (2011). *Ethics in psychotherapy and counseling: A practical guide* (4th ed.). Hoboken, NJ: Wiley. http://dx.doi.org/10.1002/9781118001875

Porfiri, L. T., & Resnick, R. J. (2000). *Law & mental health professionals: Virginia.* Washington, DC: American Psychological Association.

Roback, H. B., Moore, R. F., Bloch, F. S., & Shelton, M. (1996). Confidentiality in group psychotherapy: Empirical findings and the law. *International Journal of Group Psychotherapy, 46,* 117–135.

Rogerson, M. D., Gottlieb, M. C., Handelsman, M. M., Knapp, S., & Younggren, J. (2011). Nonrational processes in ethical decision making. *American Psychologist, 66,* 614–623. http://dx.doi.org/10.1037/a0025215

Saks, E. R., & Golshan, S. (2013). *Informed consent to psychoanalysis: The law, the theory, and the data.* New York, NY: Fordham University Press.

Sieck, B. C. (2012). Obtaining clinical writing informed consent versus using client disguise and recommendations for practice. *Psychotherapy, 49,* 3–11. http://dx.doi.org/10.1037/a0025059

Somberg, D. R., Stone, G. L., & Claiborn, C. D. (1993). Informed consent: Therapists' beliefs and practices. *Professional Psychology: Research and Practice, 24,* 153–159. http://dx.doi.org/10.1037/0735-7028.24.2.153

Sullivan, T., Martin, W. L., Jr., & Handelsman, M. M. (1993). Practical benefits of an informed-consent procedure: An empirical investigation. *Professional Psychology: Research and Practice, 24,* 160–163. http://dx.doi.org/10.1037/0735-7028.24.2.160

The Trust. (2006). *Sample outpatient services agreement for collaterals.* Retrieved from http://www.trustinsurance.com/resources/download-documents

VandeCreek, L. (2008). Considering confidentiality within broader theoretical frameworks. (Commentary on Donner, 2008). *Professional Psychology: Research and Practice, 39,* 372–373.

VandeCreek, L., & Kapp, M. B. (2005). *Law & mental health professionals: Ohio.* Washington, DC: American Psychological Association.

Wagner, L., Davis, S., & Handelsman, M. M. (1998, January). In search of the abominable consent form: The impact of readability and personalization. *Journal of Clinical Psychology, 54,* 115–120. http://dx.doi.org/10.1002/(SICI)1097-4679(199801)54:1<115::AID-JCLP13>3.0.CO;2-N

Walfish, S., & Ducey, B. B. (2007). Readability level of Health Insurance Portability and Accountability Act notices of privacy practices used by psychologists in clinical practice. *Professional Psychology: Research and Practice, 38,* 203–207. http://dx.doi.org/10.1037/0735-7028.38.2.203

Weeks, G. R., Odell, M., & Methven, S. (2005). *If only I had known . . . Avoiding common mistakes in couple therapy.* New York, NY: Norton.

Welfel, E. R., Werth, J. L., Jr., & Benjamin, G. A. H. (2009). Introduction to the duty to protect. In J. L. Werth, Jr., E. R. Welfel, & G. A. H. Benjamin (Eds.), *The duty to protect: Ethical, legal, and professional considerations for mental health professionals* (pp. 3–8). Washington, DC: American Psychological Association. http://dx.doi.org/10.1037/11866-001

Werth, J. L., Jr., Welfel, E. R., Benjamin, G. A. H., & Sales, B. D. (2009). Practice and policy responses to the duty to protect. In J. L. Werth, Jr., E. R. Welfel, & G. A. H. Benjamin (Eds.), *The duty to protect: Ethical, legal, and professional considerations for mental health professionals* (pp. 249–261). Washington, DC: American Psychological Association. http://dx.doi.org/10.1037/11866-016

Woodhouse, S. S. (2012). Clinical writing: Additional ethical and practical issues. *Psychotherapy, 49,* 22–25. http://dx.doi.org/10.1037/a0026965

Younggren, J. N., & Harris, E. A. (2008). Can you keep a secret? Confidentiality in psychotherapy. *Journal of Clinical Psychology, 64,* 589–600. http://dx.doi.org/10.1002/jclp.20480

# Index

# About the Author

**Mary Alice Fisher, PhD,** is founding director of the Center for Ethical Practice, a member of the adjunct clinical faculty at the University of Virginia, and a clinical psychologist in private practice in Charlottesville, Virginia. Dr. Fisher provides workshops, seminars, and consultation on topics related to ethical issues in clinical practice.